The Respect Effect

Leveraging Culture, Emotions and Neuroscience to Build a Better Business

Dear Jim & Jean—
Thanks so much for your years
of support and friendship!

Warm regards,

Paul
6-26-2012

By: Paul Meshanko

D1445913

First published by Legacy Business Culture

In association with:

Dog Ear Publishing
4010 W. 86th Street, Ste H
Indianapolis, IN 46268
www.dogearpublishing.net

ISBN: 978-1-4575-1202-5

This book is printed on acid-free paper.

Printed in the United States of America

Acknowledgements

Anyone who has ever gone through the process of writing a book will attest to the sacrifices that must be made both by the author and often those in his or her immediate circle of friends, family and colleagues. The completion of this book would not have been possible without the gracious support of:

- Kim, Ryan and Olivia…you guys are my reason for doing what I do!

- My staff at Legacy Business Cultures for kicking me out of the office and making it easy for me to "let go" of the business in order to write this book.

- John and Anita for the use of your "writer's retreat" in the sun.

- Nancy Traum for providing editorial structure, flexibility and support.

- Michelle, Antonia, Sidney, Deb, Melanie, Michele, Paul and everyone else who unselfishly shared their time and expertise to help with proof-reading.

I'd like to also thank all those who generously gave of their time, even on weekends, to share their stories, experiences and perceptions about this very important topic!

TABLE OF CONTENTS

Forward

Inspiration comes from many sources. I give my mother credit for my natural and never-ending curiosity about people and relationships. Working on her master's degree in theology when I was in high school, I vividly remember endless conversations with her, sometimes late into the evenings, about religious belief systems, "truths" and what happens when different belief systems collide. Combine that with my personal love of philosophy, business and neuroscience, and you have quite a mix.

I was fortunate to be mentored by some amazingly intelligent and insightful adults outside my family. One person deserves special mention. In my sophomore year of college, I was elected president of my dorm council. The dorm director was a man named Dale Linder. Dale was a black man, about six years my senior and possessed the wisdom of someone far older. To say that Dale and I clashed at times would be an understatement. Like many 20-year-olds, I had the mistaken notion that I was omnipotent; I was physically indestructible, had the world all figured out and knew exactly where I was going in life. In my ignorance, I sometimes said and did things that today make me cringe when I think back. While my specific recollection of details may be a little sketchy, I do remember Dale saying to me on multiple occasions, usually after a sigh, "Paul Meshanko, you don't know what you don't know." He was right.

When it came to dealing with people, I felt we should look past each others' differences and treat everyone the same. You know, as in the Golden Rule. I tried to put on my rose-colored glasses and pretend that we could make stereotypes, prejudices and social inequities go away just by wishing it so. I truly didn't know what I didn't know, and worse, I wasn't about to listen to anyone who suggested otherwise, including Dale. I still remember him, looking at me with a combination of frustration and determination, begging me to open my mind. He would say, "Paul, we're not all the same. If you won't acknowledge our differences and what those might mean, then you can't really respect me." Usually, my feelings would be hurt; I would get defensive and continue to insist that differences, like race, really didn't matter. In retrospect, it was my behaviors and attitudes that were hurtful. By intentionally failing to acknowledge Dale's blackness and other differences, I was treating him with disrespect.

I think it's that way with many of us. Through a combination of unintentional or purposeful ignorance, competing agendas and stubbornness, we make our way through life, sometimes treating others with disrespect along the way. The problem is that when people feel disrespected, they don't give us their best. They don't give us their attention, finest thinking and utmost effort. Fortunately, Dale had seen people like me before and demonstrated a wisdom and graciousness that at times I didn't deserve. No matter how contentious our conversations, he would always wrap up by saying, "Paul, if I didn't push you, it would mean that I didn't care about you. But I do. I care about you deeply and I want you to be successful in life." We should all be fortunate to have people like Dale in our lives. Because at some point, we all demonstrate how much we really don't know.

While neither of us could have known it at the time, those long and sometimes heated conversations with Dale planted the seeds that would eventually sprout and grow into a career and calling that I love more each day. Due to the respect with which Dale and others treated me, I graduated from college not only with a degree, but with a sense of confidence, esteem and humility. I had confidence in my thinking and ability to be a life-long learner. I learned to honor myself and be steadfast in my belief that, whatever I ended up doing in life, it would add value to this world. Most importantly, I learned humility and developed a curiosity to explore the many blind spots that would eventually, and continuously, be brought to my attention.

When I think back about Dale, I remember the movie, *Avatar*, and the line where the Na-vi acknowledged each other by saying, "I see you." Dale helped me see him as a unique individual. By seeing others as they are, black, white, short, tall, Asian, Indian, old or young, docile or angry, we acknowledge them and all that makes them unique. Only through acknowledging what they are can we then respect who they are.

INTRODUCTION

Why Focus on Respect?

Everybody's motivated by something. Likewise, there's also something that can motivate people to change. It's just a matter of figuring out what the levers are for each person. As it pertains to treating others with respect, there have historically been two important arguments that people have advocated. In recent years, additional arguments have surfaced.

According to statistics published by the American Bar Association, U.S. corporations paid $404 million in fines for various Equal Employment Opportunity Commission (EEOC) violations in 2010 and over $455 million in 2011. Frighteningly, these figures represented only fines paid for those cases that went to court and did not include attorney and other legal fees incurred. They also did not include money spent reaching settlements for claims that did not go to court. While hard data for these costs is not available because settlement details are often kept confidential, some estimates put them at over four times the actual amount of fines collected. It is safe to assume that U.S. businesses spent over $2 billion to settle claims of disrespectful, and typically unlawful, behavior. You don't have to major in finance to be impressed by the potential cost of disrespect, either individual or systemic.

The second reason used to advocate for greater respect at work is the case for social justice. Philosophically, I and many others believe there are some things that are just basically right to do. One of these things is treating others with respect and dignity, no matter who they are. The problem is that not everybody is influenced by this rationale. They may nod their heads in agreement that respect is important and that we owe it to each other, but if it doesn't impact them personally, they're not likely to change their behavior. Especially not because someone like me comes along and says it's the right thing to do.

A third reason is now emerging as a compelling motivation for focusing on respect: biology. Each of our brains is profoundly influenced by how we're treated by others. There's no smoke and mirrors here, just neurons, neurotransmitters and electrical impulses. When we're treated with respect, our brains literally light up and perform at the highest levels at which they're capable. When we're treated with disrespect, the higher thought processes in our brains go dormant. Hijacked by our primitive survival wiring, we become diminished assets to our employers and our organizations.

Linked to this third reason is yet a fourth. When we are able to create work environments that consistently value, esteem and nurture our employees, we increase something called employee engagement. Simply stated, engaged employees become emotionally committed to the success of their organizations and are much more likely to give their highest levels of discretionary effort when performing their work. In their minds, the success of their employer becomes entwined with their own personal success.

There is one final reason worth mentioning for focusing on respect: your legacy. Five or 10 years in the future, the people you interact with today aren't going to remember the exact things you said and did. Whether it was during a staff meeting, at a sales conference or on the golf course, the memories will fade. They also aren't going to remember how late you worked, what time you showed up in the morning or your spouse's name. At least most people won't, because that's not how the human brain works.

While not great at details, in most cases the brain does a superb job of recording our emotional experiences as we go through life. We remember people we met by how we typically felt when we were in their presence. If we were usually happy around them, we imagine they were smiling and kind to us. If we felt confident and proud, then we remember them guiding and supporting us. If we felt awkward, intimidated or inferior around them, we recreate their demeanor and behavior accordingly. Credit goes to the brain's limbic system for this unique methodology of remembering people and events.

Whether we realize it or not, how we engage others leaves a lasting imprint. We're literally building our own legacy in their minds, one interaction at a time. Having long since forgotten the details, people will simply remember how they felt around us and then make up the rest of the story to match. When others think of us, will they smile and fondly reminisce or will they quickly "switch channels" and find a happier memory to dwell upon? An important question to ask ourselves is how do we want to be remembered? More importantly, what are we willing to do to start responsibly building our legacy today?

PART

I

"You are not here merely to make a living. You are here in order to enable the world to live more amply, with greater vision, with a finer spirit of hope and achievement. You are here to enrich the world, and you impoverish yourself if you forget that errand."

—Woodrow Wilson

The Road to Respect

A Transformational Power

While there have been many proud moments in my career, one of the most memorable was a three-month period in 1987. I was in the second quarter of a two-term internship with the Bendix Heavy Vehicle division of AlliedSignal Corporation. I was fortunate to report to a man named Larry Taylor, who remains one of the best managers I can ever remember having. What made Larry special as a manager was that he never treated me as anything other than a fully competent associate, even though I was still a college student. His management style was to probe the outer edges of my intelligence, problem-solving skills and creativity on a continual basis.

One particular assignment still makes me smile every time I think back to it. One day, Larry said that he had an important project for me. The company was considering an acquisition and he wanted me to prepare a full strategic analysis of the companies being considered. More importantly, he asked that I come back to him with a recommendation once the analysis was complete. I remember feeling both excited and frightened. For a kid still in college, this was the kind of project that would require me to pull from every business discipline I had been exposed to up until that point.

The project itself took almost two months to complete. In the end, I presented a full analysis of three potential acquisition targets, including their financial strength, market position, reputation within our industry and range of products and services. While all three companies were attractive candidates, there was one that stood out to me as clearly being the best target. My analysis and recommendations, including multiple graphs and charts, took the form of a 60-page report with my name squarely on the cover page. I still remember walking in Larry's office, handing it to him, and proudly saying, "Here you go." At that time, it represented not only a meaningful departure from term papers and case studies, but also the best work I was capable of producing.

Later that afternoon, my desk phone rang and Larry asked me to come to his office. He said, "I have reviewed your report and recommendation and it is excellent. It's so good that I have already sent it to Dave and would like you to present it to him in person tomorrow." Dave was Larry's boss and responsible for all aftermarket strategy and marketing for our group. This level of recognition for my work, and its implied confidence in me, was somewhat unexpected. What an impact it had! The euphoria and motivation it instilled in me lasted for years. It set the stage for me to accept the company's offer to work for them as a full-time employee once I graduated from college even though I had two offers at a slightly higher starting salary.

> *"As we look ahead into the next century, leaders will be those who empower others."*
>
> —Bill Gates

Looking back through the 25-year-lens-of-experience, it's only now that I fully appreciate the complex and powerful forces put into play that year. More than anything, Larry primed my emotional pump by treating me in a manner that made me feel smart, capable and important. He also helped me feel like I was part of the team and see how my contributions played an integral part in the long-term strategic and financial success of the business. While he probably didn't realize it at the time, his intentional and consistent demonstration of respect for me as a person and young professional helped set in motion the productive and rewarding trajectory for the first 10 years of my professional career. Because of his communication of confidence in me, I developed a powerful emotional tie to both my boss and the company. Whether it's a project, acquisition or purchase of equipment, either mentally or physically businesses map their return on investment (ROI). In this case, the investment was in me, and the return was the maximum engagement of my skills for the betterment of the company. What can a company do to maximize the return on investment it's made in its employees? A good starting place is to make respect an integral part of the company's corporate culture.

Our Literal Connection to Each Other

One of the most fascinating perspectives I've read recently was in Daniel Goleman's book, *Primal Leadership*[1]. Goleman refers to human beings as "open loop systems." From an evolutionary perspective, our species is more connected to each other than we realize. Over the course of our evolution, human beings developed highly specialized brain circuitry that monitors other people when we're in their presence. In psychology, it's referred to as Theory of Mind, the ability to identify mental states such as beliefs in ourselves and others, and to realize those beliefs can be different from ours. Our brains can then do their best to understand other people's intentions. At a basic level, think of it as each of us having our own, personal threat detection system.

> *"The emotional brain responds to an event more quickly than the thinking brain."*
>
> —Daniel Goleman

From an evolutionary perspective, this makes complete sense. The ability to predict accurately the peaceful or hostile intentions of new people or animals, literally, promoted the longevity of our species. What is fascinating about this circuitry is that it's forever in the "on" mode. What this means is that we're always monitoring other people around us and they're doing the same. Our conclusions about the intentions of others have a profound effect on how the rest of our brain functions. Informed by inputs from our five senses, our brains perform a delicate and instinctual dance every day in the name of self-preservation.

Armed with this complex warning system, the human brain is the world's most sophisticated survival computer ever developed. Whenever our senses pick up cues that could indicate that we are or could be in the presence of danger, ancient neural pathways activate to get us out of harm's way as quickly and effectively as possible. This is the realm of fight or flight. So powerful are these impulses that they literally commandeer the brain and order all other non-essential thinking functions to go dormant. This means that all of our higher-order brain capabilities, such as problem solving, reasoning, evaluating alternatives, planning, socializing and empathizing are subordinated to protecting ourselves in the presence of perceived threats. This includes more than just physical threats; it also includes threats to our emotional well-being, social status, financial security and future opportunities.

Conversely, when we interpret cues from others to mean that we are safe in their midst, our higher-level thought processes go back on-line and we return to a normal level of thinking and intellectual/operational output. This "all systems safe" mode of brain function is hopefully where most of us spend the majority of our waking hours getting things done for our employers, families and selves.

From a workplace perspective, there is a mode that's more beneficial and desirable than "all systems safe." It is the mode in which we function when we perceive ourselves to be free from danger and in the presence of those who appreciate us, value what we contribute and deem our best effort as being essential to the overall success of the group. It is also the mode in which we are constructively challenged, given opportunities and resources to be successful, and can share in the rewards of our collaboration with others. When we operate in this type of rich, stimulating and emotionally nourishing environment, our brains are more productive than normal. They release powerful neurotransmitters that stimulate our creativity, desire to work collaboratively and allow us to find deep personal satisfaction in our work. This is the *Respect Effect*.

The Neurology of Human Interaction

Human evolution and biology play significant roles in determining how we interact and behave around each other. Powered almost exclusively by glucose, the form of sugar our bodies metabolize from carbohydrates, our brains are wired for speed and efficiency. Because we have limited supplies of glucose available throughout the day, one of our natural, and often unacknowledged, biases is to stay in environments that are familiar and use neural pathways that are already well-developed. When we're surrounded by people who are like us (or at least very familiar to us), we spend less glucose (energy) to understand their actions and predict their intentions. This preference for familiarity, predictability and safety is likely one of the underlying factors that drove our ancestors to form tribes.

When we're around people for whom we have no first-hand reference points, our brains immediately try to match what we can perceive about them (visually, audibly and through our sense of smell) to patterns that already exist. According to authors Marsh, Mendoza-Denton and Smith:

> "Neuroscience has shown that people can identify another person's apparent race, gender, and age in a matter of milliseconds. In this blink of an eye, a complex network of stereotypes, emotional prejudices, and behavioral impulses activates."[2]

These mental shortcuts allow us to quickly evaluate people, and our relative safety around them. There is strong evidence that they also permit the brain to consume less of the body's precious supply of glucose. When we have no existing reference points for a person, event or situation, the brain must work harder and burn considerably more energy to program new neuronal reference points and synaptic pathways. Think of it as the difference between driving down a highway versus having to build that highway in the first place. Once our "highways" are built, we are comfortable staying on them as much as possible. To a degree, this analogy helps underscore the power and persistence of stereotypes to influence our perceptions and initial interaction behaviors with others.

What Is Respect?

The word respect has its origins in the Latin noun respectus, which translates literally to: the act of looking back, and the Latin verb, respicere, which means to look back. Today, the actual word, as it pertains to people, has evolved to be defined by Merriam-Webster the following ways:

> Respect: noun - 1) the act of giving particular attention: consideration, 2) high or special regard: esteem, 3) the quality of being esteemed.
>
> Respect: verb - 1a) to consider worthy of high regard: esteem, 2) to refrain from interfering with, 3) to have reference to: concern.

Acquiring enormous scope the word has gradually morphed to mean different things since its first use in the 14th century. What makes the word so important is that, when experienced, it triggers powerful, positive emotions that not only feel good but change our behaviors. Of critical significance is that these emotional responses seem to be universal. While the actions and decisions that trigger the feeling of being respected will vary from person to person and culture to culture, the core emotion is experienced identically in all human beings. Respect *feels* the same way, no matter your age, race, gender, religion, level of intelligence or ability. Similarly, the neurological responses to being treated with respect appear to be universal. We will explore these later.

A forward-looking definition

I'd like to suggest the following as a reference point for further exploring respect as a cultural component:

> *Respect is an active process of non-judgmentally engaging people from all backgrounds. It is practiced to increase our awareness and effectiveness, and demonstrated in a manner that esteems both us and those with whom we interact.*

One implication of this definition is that it doesn't permit complacency or a status quo level of social comfort. The genuine pursuit of respect requires effort, takes time and will likely feel awkward at times as we push ourselves to engage people from whom we have historically kept our distance. Neurologically, the more different from us others appear, the more energy our brains have to spend to categorize and make sense of the differences. Part of this mental effort is spent creating new neural pattern circuits. Another part is spent turning down the volume of our inner voices that want to use shortcuts to process the differences.

When defining respect, the inclusion of esteem also deserves discussion. Whether or not our interactions with others have been successful in conveying respect will depend on the emotional state of others after interacting with us. If our efforts have succeeded, the desired result is for those we interact with to feel valued in some way, as colleagues, co-workers, friends, neighbors or simply as people. When we make ourselves partially responsible for the emotional well-being of those around us, it enhances our own sense of esteem. Think of it as the "pay it forward" effect.

What this definition does *not* mean is that all of our conversations with others will be pleasant and that difficult situations can't be discussed. It's quite the opposite. This definition of respect actually requires that we engage in candid conversations with individuals with whom we have problems. If an employee who reports to us is not performing at the required level, it is critical that we share this information with them. In order to maintain or build esteem in a person whose performance is inadequate, it is important that we separate the person from their performance. We can give candid feedback about their performance while letting the individual know that we value them as a person and want them to succeed. Even more impactful is making it clear that our intent is to do whatever we can to help them become successful. From the perspective of the person receiving feedback, they are more willing to hear critical feedback about their performance provided they feel cared about as a person and that someone is committed to helping them meet their requirements.

Respect is not tolerance

Imagine that your spouse, partner or significant other came home from work one Friday afternoon and, with a smile on his or her face, enthusiastically declared that they loved their job because their boss and co-workers *tolerated* them. We would probably look at them as if they had a screw loose because the feeling of being tolerated and their expression of joy didn't match! Most people don't associate the feeling of being tolerated with overt happiness, smiles and energy. That's not to say that tolerance is bad; it's simply a mediocre standard given the alternatives. Think of it as receiving a rating of "average" on your performance review. It's not an unsatisfactory, but it doesn't put your workplace performance at a level that can lead to a personal and/or monetary reward.

Whenever we interact with others, either at work or in our private lives, there is a broad range of possible behaviors that we can demonstrate (see The Road to Respect.) Tolerating others is a neutral position. It is not positive or negative in its impact and requires little energy to initiate and sustain. That's why people typically perceive themselves as being tolerant. When surveyed, most people indicate that they are more tolerant than those around them (the "better than average" effect.) We would find it difficult to refute these internal, and usually unspoken, beliefs because the demonstration of tolerance has few behaviors or actions associated with it. The possible exception is when we are around others who we perceive to be annoying. Then tolerance requires more effort.

The Island of Misfit Toys

If you've ever eaten at a Hard Rock Cafe, one of the first things that made an impression on you was the outstanding collection of rock 'n roll memorabilia gracing the walls. The next thing you noticed is the equally memorable collection of stage-ready staffers employed by Hard Rock to provide you with a remarkable dining experience. Tattoos, body piercings, Mohawks or spiked hair in all colors with clothes to match, can create an almost uneasy feeling for first-time Hard Rock patrons. My first visit in 2009 (Baltimore, MD) was no different. That is, until I was greeted with a huge smile, amazingly friendly attitude and a simple welcome, "Hi, my name is Gordon, and I'll be your server today. Have you ever eaten at a Hard Rock before?" As I sat in our booth with my wife and young kids waiting for my response, I cautiously said, "No, this is our first time." Gordon beamed. "Cool! You're going to love it here. By the way, only my parents call me Gordon. You can call me Sly!" With that, my apprehensions vanished.

According to Jim Knight, Sr., Director of Training and Development for Hard Rock International, the previously described and authentic greeting is what sets the tone for an amazing guest experience. It's also part of the Hard Rock's unique formula for success in an industry that each year sees a higher-than-average failure rate for new entrants. It is part of the same formula that propelled the company to legendary patron status and solid financial performance since Americans Peter Morton and Isaac Tigrett opened the first restaurant in London, England in 1971.

The Hard Rock guest experience starts with the hiring process for their distinctive staff. Knight has a direct hand in training the majority of management personnel within the organization. "We're kind of like the Island of Misfit Toys from the television Christmas special," he grinned during a recent interview in Orlando, Florida. "We look to hire employees who, because of their individuality, might not fit in with more traditional restaurants." He went on to say, "There's something special about the chemistry between our staffers because they're all kind of outsiders in some way or another. The Hard Rock guest experience is a direct result of this *we're all freaks* chemistry. It kind of results in a flavor of teamwork and commitment that, quite honestly, I've never seen matched in other hospitality-related organizations."

The spike-haired and energetic Knight modestly tried to minimize his own influence. When pressed, he acknowledged his hands-on style of training and development content for Hard Rock managers. The element that appears to be most important is an emphasis on creating a "rock star" experience for customers and employees. This approach is obviously a winner because the chain boasts patron evaluations that are best-in-class, and a staff turnover that is half the industry average. To an outsider looking in, the connection seems obvious.

Knight has been part of the Hard Rock team for over 20 years. What keeps him there? It's more than the Rolex watch - each employee, no matter what their position, gets one after 10 years. It's more than the travel and knowing he's personally making a difference. Reflecting on the company's underlying approach, *Do well by doing well,* he said, "This place is kind of in my DNA. I love what I do, love the people I do it with and love the guests we all do it for." On the wall directly behind Knight's head is one of the several short sayings for which the Hard Rock Cafe is so famous – *LOVE ALL – SERVE ALL*®.

Once we move away from the relatively passive mode of simply tolerating others, we start exerting energy, typically mental and occasionally physical. We start *behaving* around others in relation to our perceptions of what their presence signifies. Those behaviors are predicated on our stored knowledge, including the stereotypes that we have about them or people like them. Here's where our evolutionary instincts come into the equation. Our first genetically imprinted directive is to remain safe. People feel safest when they are around others who are like them. The problem is that given the vast range of dissimilarities between people, we perceive most people as different from us. A colleague suggested to me years ago that many of us unintentionally alienate ourselves from others merely by our self-perceived sense of "terminal uniqueness."

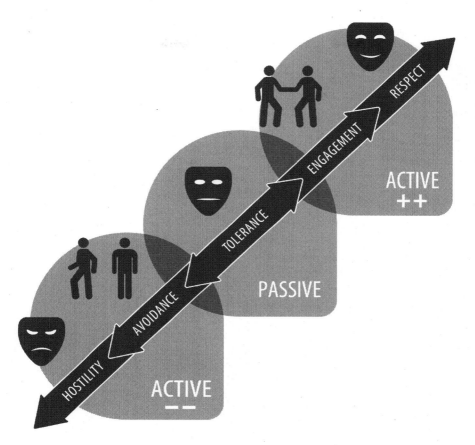

When we perceive that we are interacting with unfamiliar people who have unknown or suspect motives, the natural emotion that surfaces is suspicion (or minimally, caution). The behavioral manifestation of suspicion is avoidance. The same response can be expected when we are in the presence of people for whom we have stereotyped information that suggests unpredictable or hostile intentions. Over the course of our evolution, this "play it safe" response kept our ancestors out of harm's way and increased our chances of long-term survival. In situations where the presence of unfamiliar people suggests impending conflict or danger, our level of physical and mental energy usage goes up beyond avoidance. We prepare ourselves to initiate or protect ourselves from hostility.

Life today is very different from the world in which our prehistoric ancestors fought for survival. While there are occasional situations in which we perceive physical danger, potentially dangerous people are more likely to threaten us with psychological, emotional or social harm. That's why the term *hostility* needs to be defined broadly.

> Hostile behavior is an intentional activity that harms another person in any way, including physically, emotionally, socially, financially, professionally or by reputation. Hostility can also be demonstrated by behaviors that intentionally impede others in meeting their predetermined goals.

For those employed in workplaces where hostile behaviors are openly tolerated or even encouraged, there is little doubt to the damage inflicted on productivity. Energy spent perpetrating or deflecting hostility is energy that can't be spent doing the work individuals were hired to do.

Hostile behaviors are at the polar opposite end of the spectrum from behaviors associated with respect. The question is what will send our behavior in a different direction, away from avoidance and hostility and towards *engagement*. The answer is remarkably simple. While initially not easy, selectively rewiring our brains to respond to differences with *curiosity* instead of suspicion is the most direct path. When practiced, cultivating an attitude of curiosity about the differences between ourselves and others leads to an entirely different set of behaviors and actions. When we're curious about something or someone, rather than avoiding them, we should engage them to explore the differences. It is this active demonstration of curiosity that leads us to explore the unique individuality that differentiates us from others. It is also the path that leads us to discover similarities that may not be visible on the surface and, ultimately, to respect.

The benefits of curiosity notwithstanding, it would be naïve to think that there was never a place for suspicion in our world. Not every situation or person is safe to be around. To walk alone at night in a part of town that has a statistically higher incidence of physical crime would be foolhardy. Similarly, letting your guard down around a person who treated you with hostility in the past would be unwise. No species would survive if it completely ignored known threats to its safety and well-being.

An attitude of curiosity starts with the intention to exit our familiar orbit and subordinate our more primal fear of the unknown. But there has to be a value proposition for doing so; a future benefit linked to learning more about others or we won't exert the effort required to refocus our attention. A degree of mindfulness is also helpful; being observant when our minds initially tell us to be careful and being able to push back gently with reason and ask ourselves, "What is the danger?"

As we learn to turn down the volume of our own "noise," we become more aware of stories about other people and their imagined intentions. This is part of our explanatory style, our ability to explain to ourselves why we experience a particular event, either positive or negative. Uncovering and owning our current stories, even the unpleasant ones, allows us to begin to test them through reason and a fresh outlook. Do our apprehensions and suspicions make sense logically or are they simply leftover artifacts from inherited stereotypes and past experiences that are too old to be relied upon accurately to predict the future?

> *"If you have some respect for people as they are, you can be more effective in helping them to become better than they are."*
>
> —John W. Gardner

While more tangible benefits typically come later, curiosity leads to a process of discovery that is intrinsically enjoyable and valuable. When we mutually make the time to get to know others at levels beyond what the senses can detect, there is a co-validation that takes place for all parties. Some cultures have a specific vocabulary to describe this process. In Bantu (African), it's sometimes referred to as *Ubuntu* (pronounced oo-BUUN-too), "I am what I am because of who we all are." *Namaste* (pronounced NAH-m s-tay) from India translates to, "The spirit in me respects the spirit in you." When we acknowledge and validate each other, we become connected and a part of something bigger. This discovery process, taking varying degrees of effort, leads us to the doorstep of respect.

Making a Difference with Mutual Respect

In the summer of 2010, Medical Mutual of Ohio launched Mutual Respect, an initiative that would build on the company's already-strong employee satisfaction ratings and turn it into an active force to improve areas, including customer service, employee commitment and trust. According to Tom Greene, VP of Human Resources, "The goal of any program of this type should be to create an environment that, over time, will continue to foster retention, improve employee continuity and make for a better customer experience. All of those characteristics help differentiate Medical Mutual in the marketplace."

Support for the idea came straight from the top. The board of directors of Medical Mutual recognized that their people were their company's greatest competitive advantage. Patty Hartmann, Manager of Corporate Learning and Development, noted that both the board and senior leadership wanted to leverage the company's diversity, not as a passive way to recognize people's differences, but to use them actively to make Medical Mutual stronger. "We knew we had a culture that understood diversity and supported differences," said Hartmann, "but we wanted to turn that into a competitive asset that helped us succeed in the market. It's the next step in continuing to build an inclusive culture."

Medical Mutual officially launched Mutual Respect by first surveying all 2,700 of its employees in Ohio, Indiana, South Carolina and Georgia to establish internal benchmark data on perceptions of respectfulness in the culture. According to Sandy Opacich, Director of HR, "We have been doing employee satisfaction surveys for several years, but with Edge Ohio on board, we were able to interweave questions developed specifically to ascertain the level of respect within." The initial survey response rate was 70%, which was substantial. The results showed that, while Medical Mutual was already perceived as a respectful work environment, there was room for improvement in some key areas.

Acting on data and insights gained from the survey process, Medical Mutual quickly followed up with a customized training curriculum designed to position respect as a platform for better understanding the broader concept of diversity and how to leverage it for culture change. Their training partner was quick to point out that an authentic culture of respect goes beyond the traditional [diversity] focus on awareness of differences. While this may be a good starting point, authentic respect requires the active commitment of all managers and employees to treat each other in ways that build esteem and communicate value.

Initially, a half-day workshop was delivered to all leaders and managers, including the chief executive officer. Following the management workshops, each manager was required to work with his or her team members to facilitate the creation of a Code of Cooperation. These "living guidelines" typically included 8-12 behaviorally specific statements detailing how employees who work together agreed to engage with and treat each other. What sets Mutual Respect apart from past diversity efforts, according to Medical Mutual's Tom Greene, is that, "The results of the survey and the manager-level training include a clear link to organization-wide efforts to foster a culture of respect."

With management already having completed the program, Medical Mutual is now offering over 30 sessions of the Mutual Respect workshop to all employees on a voluntary basis. Their business partner has certified internal staff to facilitate the workshop and Hartmann says it has been very well attended. "So far, all sessions have been full, most with waiting lists," she says. "We re-surveyed our employees in third-quarter 2011 and, judging by the results, we do see a definite connection between perceptions of respect and other metrics, like retention, which have a measurable impact on our company."

Why Respect Matters

In order to understand the potential respect has for unleashing the best in an organization, we first have to recognize what it does at the individual level. There are all sorts of behaviors, many that vary from culture to culture and even from person to person, that may trigger the emotional feeling of respect in the recipient. Here are just a few:

- Offering a verbal compliment
- Giving them public recognition
- Including them in an important discussion
- Making direct eye contact
- Seeking their opinion on an important matter
- Asking them for assistance
- Supporting their work and objectives
- Offering assistance to help them succeed
- Referring to their opinion and expertise
- Addressing them by their first name
- Showing an interest in their work
- Showing and interest in their family
- Showing concern for their health & well-being
- Giving them your undivided attention
- Validating their opinions and ideas
- Sharing your limited resources
- Referring or recommending them to others
- Being completely candid
- Making a personal sacrifice for them
- Defending them in front of others
- Empathizing with set-back or loss

What's interesting about these behaviors and their supporting entourage of verbal and nonverbal cues is that they all have the potential to evoke strong, positive emotion. More specifically, they trigger the release of powerful and pleasurable chemicals in our brains that we interpret as positive emotions. Dr. Ellen Weber, Director, MITA Brain Based Center, was recently quoted in *HR Magazine*:

> "Social fairness and respect help employees learn. When we show interest in others, support them and praise them genuinely, we 'squirt' a chemical mix of serotonin and oxytocin into their brains. These neurotransmitters encourage trust, open others' minds to our ideas, and create desire to get to know us better and to help with whatever we need done."[3]

Over the years, I've queried literally thousands of participants on the emotions that surface when they are treated with respect. Here is just a small sampling of their responses:

- Happy
- Validated
- Important
- Energized
- Part of the group
- Safe
- Intelligent
- Motivated
- Engaged
- Committed
- Inspired to work even harder
- Accepted
- Vital
- Honored
- Proud
- Needed
- Trusted
- Valued

On its surface, this feel-good list of emotions looks nice. But, does it make a difference in the quality and quantity of work people do? To answer the question, imagine that when you leave your home to go to work each day, you take an invisible backpack that contains all your emotions. When you arrive at work, your backpack probably contains emotions that were generated by your commute. Rather than leaving this backpack in your locker or desk, you carry it with you throughout the day. Every time you interact with someone, the contents of the backpack change to reflect the emotional quality of your interaction.

Do these emotions cause a change? When asked, the vast majority of respondents answered in the affirmative. The universal response I have received on five continents can be summarized this way: *In the presence of these emotions, we are likely to be doing the very best work we are capable of for our organizations.* That level of effort can translate into significant organizational advantages. Here are a few:

Higher job satisfaction and employee engagement.

When people are consistently treated with respect by colleagues and co-workers, they enjoy being at work and are more likely to become emotionally committed to the success of their organization. Research conducted by the Gallup organization, among others, has linked elevated levels of employee engagement to significantly higher levels of productivity and profitability when compared to businesses in the same industry that have lower levels of engagement.[4]

Employee engagement is different from employee satisfaction, and is a better indicator of the emotional connection employees have to their organizations. Dr. Paul Marciano made the following observation:

"Indeed, engagement is all about commitment; the word comes from the Old French (en +gage) meaning 'to pledge oneself'." Although not quite so life altering, the concept of employee engagement is also about the extent to which one is committed, dedicated and loyal to one's organization, supervisor, work and colleagues. When you're truly committed, motivation becomes a lot less relevant - you're in it for the long haul.[5]

Improved physical and emotional health of associates.

Employees who can count on and anticipate respectful interactions at work are typically beneficiaries of better physical health. Dr. Michael Roizen from the Cleveland Clinic suggests that, with very few exceptions, the quality of our relationships with others is an even greater predictor of our physical health than our personal lifestyles and habits.[6]

Improved ability to attract, develop and retain talented employees.

When work places have a reputation for being consistently respectful, they also tend to be more fun, energetic and collaborative. These are the qualities that make businesses attractive to both potential and current employees. Innovative companies are finding that they need to spend less money and time searching for new employees because their own "cultural brand" sells itself. Potential employees seek these businesses for employment opportunities, and current employees become active in recruiting new employees. Engaged, happy and productive employees tend to want to surround themselves with other people like themselves.

Improved information flow and organizational learning.

You don't have to pry information loose from people in respectful workplaces. Freely sharing information important to the business is commonplace. Competitor and customer updates come in from the field and are quickly shared with other parts of the organization. Opinions, suggestions and observations about strategy are shared without reservation. Problems and setbacks are openly discussed and collaboratively resolved.

Improved customer satisfaction.

Smiles are contagious, even over the phone. Employees who are consistently treated with respect tend to maintain happier, friendlier dispositions. They are prone to making themselves emotionally available and empathetic to the needs of their customers and clients. Customers, including patients, who feel their service providers genuinely care about trying to help them are more likely to remain customers. They also frequently share their positive views with others.

Higher organizational productivity, profitability and resilience.

One of the biggest benefits we gain from creating respectful workplaces is that we increase our bandwidth or ability to successfully engage in more than one thing at a time. More energy and commitment are available for creativity, innovation and problem-solving when employees and managers are emotionally healthy. We bring our best selves to work and take great pride in utilizing our talents for the betterment of the company. A good word to describe this type of work environment is authentic. When we create emotionally safe environments that allow all employees to be authentic, to comfortably bring their entire selves to work, we free up incredible energy that might otherwise be used to protect or defend.

Even in times of change, employees who work in respectful workplaces find it easier to work collaboratively to accomplish what needs to be done. This is due to the level of trust that exists between people. When individuals know that the people they work with "have their backs" and can be trusted to support them, they focus more of their energies on managing changes in the environment instead of on their relationships.

Respect – The Invisible Force Behind Zappos

In a small, downtown Las Vegas coffee shop, Tony Hsieh, founder of online super-retailer Zappos, thoughtfully shared his opinion on the power of respect. As captured in his best selling book, *Delivering Happiness*, he identified Zappos' 10 core values as the foundation for the company's success. Curiously, not one of the values explicitly mentions the word *respect.* How could Zappos create a path to profits, passion and purpose without an emphasis on respect? "You can't," answered Hsieh.

As a company, Zappos understands exactly how important culture is to both the employees and the long-term success of the business. Hsieh explained, "Culture is to a company as communities are to a city." Indeed, his hobby is to study the great cities of the world and analyze their growth patterns. He continued, "When a city doubles in size, the culture doesn't die, it evolves." When Zappos moved from San Francisco to Las Vegas in 2003, the company had only 60 employees. Today, the number exceeds 1,300. The core cultural elements that propelled its start-up years ago are still the ones that help it consistently rank as one of the best places to work by Forbes. Zappos is on the move again, and in 2013 will take over the old City Hall building in downtown Las Vegas. Success will surely follow.

Every year, Zappos asks its employees to email their responses to a single question: "What does the Zappos culture mean to you?" The unedited responses are then combined and published in the Zappos Culture Book. Like an annual rite of passage, this document has become a cornerstone for helping current employees communicate and perpetuate the culture that has made the company so successful. Even customers and vendors can weigh in. One recently wrote, "The Zappos culture is all about respect. Respect for their employees, vendors and, most importantly, customers." In some cases, employees share deeply personal stories. One entry in the 2011 edition read, "Zappos has changed my life. Every day, I am around people who respect each other and are not afraid to be themselves..." When asked how entries such as these made him feel, Hsieh said, "I guess if they didn't say those things I would be sad."

With sales topping $1 billion in 2009, and a recent acquisition by Amazon promising more of the same in the future, Zappos has continued to evolve. And just like the cities Hsieh has studied, growth means change. The company was recently split into 10 separate business units, each still committed to the core values required for *Delivering Happiness*. Curiously, this includes helping other organizations find their own path to profits, passion and purpose. "Respect is, in a way, the foundation for our culture, and now we intentionally share that with others." Tony continued, "Without respect in our workplace, Zappos simply would not be here today."

The final question for Tony had to do with how he and other leaders within Zappos handle any complaints of disrespect in their workplace. He quickly replied, "If it cannot be successfully handled within the workgroup, we fire them." Zero tolerance for disrespect is one of the ways that respect has become an ingrained part of the Zappos culture - without it ever being mentioned by name.

The Aftermath of Disrespect

Just as respect triggers a complex release of neurotransmitters that bring about certain emotions, disrespect does the same. The results, however, are considerably different. In preparation for writing this book, I put the word out through my network of friends and colleagues that I was in search of stories of disrespect. I didn't want to hear about the occasional and soon forgotten behavioral blemishes. I wanted stories that were etched into memories and still, after many years, evoked emotion.

My personal story involved a former strategic partner. Working with a long-term client for several months, I created an opening for one of our partners to provide their services through our company. The effort culminated with us making an on-site sales call at the client's headquarters in Virginia. The call was spectacularly successful and we ended up winning a contract worth almost $250,000. Even though most of that would go to our partner, I was thrilled with the outcome because my client was happy. More importantly, the path was set for future collaboration.

Unfortunately, what started out as a successful venture soon fell apart. Shortly after the sales call, "Steve," the VP of Sales for our partner, called me on the phone and laid into me with a display of foul language, name-calling and accusations that left me speechless. Evidently, I took too much of the lead in the call for his liking. I had positioned myself into the subsequent client management activities more than he wanted, even though it was my customer. For good measure, he finished his assault by criticizing my personal sales skills as not being aggressive enough in promoting my services.

> *"When once the forms of civility are violated, there remains little hope of return to kindness or decency."*
>
> —Samuel Johnson

About 30 seconds into the call, I distinctly remember having an almost out-of-body experience, wondering if the conversation was really taking place. No warning, no gradual escalation of emotion, just a verbal ambush and with no place for me to hide. My brain locked down and I was powerless. Was this an anomaly or was this Steve's typical behavior? Was he under stress and this was how he normally responded when things didn't go his way? It didn't matter at that point. While Steve was relatively new in his position, I had worked with his company's founders for several years. The entire relationship was compromised in that 90-second conversation. We eventually won the contract, and that was the last time I ever introduced that partner to one of my clients. I intentionally hired an employee shortly after that incident that had the skill set necessary to bring that company's core service offering in-house. They are now a major profit center for my business.

This example demonstrates how quickly disrespect can destroy something that took years to build. In this case, the primary casualty was trust. While Steve may have had some valid points, whatever those were and my willingness to consider them were lost because of the way his message was delivered. His attacking style put me immediately on the defensive and literally short-circuited the parts of my brain that are responsible for reflection and evaluation. It is important to note that I didn't just lose trust in Steve. I also lost trust in those who hired him and never did business with them again.

The Damage Runs Deep

In addition to my story, I have had workshop participants from all levels within an organization share stories about having been treated with disrespect. Shop floor workers, customer service associates, front-line supervisors and senior leaders all had stories about being treated poorly. Some of the incidents happened years ago. The greater the degree of perceived disrespect, the more quickly and vividly the incidents were recalled.

Here is just a short list of some of the damaging behaviors that were shared:

- Was lied to
- Was referred to by an ethnic slur
- Was subjected to sexual innuendo
- Was excluded from important meeting
- Was the subject of gossip
- Was cursed and yelled at
- Had their idea laughed at publicly
- Manager took credit for their idea
- Was blamed for someone else's error
- Was intentionally excluded from social activities
- Was routinely interrupted and talked over
- Was spoken to in a condescending manner
- Was subjected to gender stereotyping
- Was verbally taunted
- Was held to a different standard than peers
- Was propositioned even though married
- Was subjected to proselytizing
- Was told they were too old to be promoted
- Was told they were not promotable because of the college they attended
- Had their physical attributes discussed publicly
- Was subjected to eye rolls, sighs and other dis-respectful nonverbal signals
- Was told they dressed funny
- Had their confidential comments made public
- Was told to "get a clue" by their boss
- Was expected to reply to routine text messages late at night

- Had their boss skip an important meeting to go golfing
- Was told to shut up by their supervisor in front of their peers
- Had an interviewee interrupt the interview to respond to a text
- Had boss interrupt annual performance review to call his stock broker

What's interesting about these disrespectful behaviors is that the damage they caused often wasn't restricted to the direct recipient. When we observe someone treating another person disrespectfully, we make a note of it. It is part of our self-preservation wiring. The offending individual wasn't treating us poorly but it could be our turn in the future. When we see the capacity for the disrespectful behavior in another person, we take note and are likely to keep that individual at arm's length so we don't become their next victim. The greater the authority a person has in an organization, the more damage they can do. A senior leader who is permitted to treat underlings with routine disrespect because it is "their style" can cause tremendous damage to trust and morale within the organization. The reason these behaviors are so damaging is because the negative emotions that result have the potential to undermine both individual and group productivity.

The damage starts with a chemical release of two potent hormones, adrenaline and cortisol. Both molecules occur naturally in the body and, in small doses, play an important role in keeping us safe. The problem is that our brains don't distinguish between physical and emotional safety. The electro-chemical warning systems that responded when our prehistoric ancestors were attacked by a saber tooth tiger or predatory tribe are the same ones that activate to protect us from an attacking dog, a swerving car or an assailant with a gun. Our brain also responds similarly to verbal attacks, taunting, being publicly embarrassed and receiving threatening e-mail messages. The release of cortisol and adrenaline cause the brain to focus exclusively on self protection. In this mode, the brain shuts down a region called the prefrontal cortex that is responsible for coordinating our executive functions such as reasoning, maintaining attention, managing our impulses, evaluating alternatives and solving problems.

When we treat people in the workplace in ways they perceive to be disrespectful, we deactivate the parts of their brains that are capable of performing the tasks they were hired to complete. We temporarily take them off-line as human assets of the business. Depending on how severe the response, it may take up to four hours for the cortisol levels to return to normal. Even then, the damage isn't over. Every time the individual replays the mental tape of the occurrence, the same chemical response is initiated by the brain. The purpose of this response is as basic as it is unstoppable: to reinforce the brain's memory of the danger and protect the individual from a similar kind of attack in the future.

Here is a sample of the many emotions that individuals have reported feeling when they were treated with disrespect and their protection circuits were activated:

- Attacked
- Angry
- Confused
- Sabotaged
- Embarrassed
- Frustrated

- Inadequate
- Incompetent
- Hopeless
- Trapped
- Depressed
- Spiteful
- Humiliated
- Insecure
- Excluded
- Unmotivated
- Disengaged
- Paralyzed
- Fearful
- Unimportant
- Defensive

How do these emotions affect the quality of our work, both individually and as a whole? Let's return to the backpack analogy. Imagine going to work. By midday your backpack contains a few of the emotions listed above and you're now carrying them wherever you go. What would be the quality of your work? What would be your motivation to do your best work? When I ask this of workshop participants, I go to great lengths to make sure it is not a rhetorical question. After a few awkward moments of silence, someone finally speaks up and typically says, "We're not doing any work. We're just going through the motions." Even if we wanted to, our brains are physically incapable of doing their best work because they are spending a great portion of their available energy in protection mode.

When people ask me what types of organizations employ our company, I like to answer that there are two kinds. The first are companies proactively planning and working to create respectful workplaces so they are able to get the maximum contribution from each employee. The second kind are organizations for whom the proverbial "horse has already gotten out of the barn." Somehow, a pattern of disrespectful behaviors has taken root and damage has occurred. With these clients, we see the following productivity-related challenges:

Low employee engagement levels.

When employees are not engaged, they are less likely to give discretionary effort on behalf of their employer. The performance of work becomes a simple monetary transaction in which they generate whatever is perceived to be the lowest level of effort required to collect their paycheck.

Higher rates of stress-related illnesses within employee and leadership ranks.

One of the more intriguing medical research discoveries in recent years is the connection between stress hormones and cardiovascular disease. Employees in disrespectful workplaces are more likely to show elevated levels of adrenaline and cortisol. While some levels of these compounds are necessary to keep us safe, long-term, continual exposure can result in blood vessel lesions that eventually scar over and attract plaque. Over time, this significantly raises the susceptibility to cardiovascular disease. This phenomenon occurs both with humans and other primate species. It doesn't take a tremendous leap in logic to hypothesize that disrespectful workplaces may actually end up causing their owners and workers higher health care costs.

One particularly damaging demonstration of hostility is a form of bullying that occurs when certain peers are intentionally excluded from group-related activities. Oftentimes, this behavior starts with either work-related or social activities and then extends to the other over time. According to a recent study highlighted in the *Journal of Management*:

> *Workplace ostracism, an adult form of bullying, is often described as an individual's belief that they are ignored or excluded by superiors or colleagues in the workplace. A 2005 survey of 262 full-time employees found that over a five-year period, 66% of respondents felt they were systematically ignored by colleagues, and 29% reported that other people intentionally left the area when they entered. Previous studies have shown that ostracism is an interpersonal stressor that can lead to psychological distress. Workplace distress is strongly linked to life distress, employee turnover and poor physical health.* [7]

Higher levels of absenteeism.

When employees have low perceptions of how they are treated by their peers and supervisors, they are more likely to call in sick when they are marginally ill. We've all had those days when we think to ourselves, "I don't feel that well. Should I go to work or not?" Those who work in disrespectful work environments are less likely to go to work.

Higher rates of workplace accidents.

A trusted colleague of mine was formerly the director of safety for a large petroleum and chemical company. He shared with me that there was a definite connection between accidents and workplace culture. When people are treated disrespectfully, they often end up working with head and hands in different places. Quite literally, they perform their jobs without fully paying attention to what they're doing because they may be processing how to protect themselves from disrespectful treatment.

Above industry average employee turnover rates.

While not an immediate threat, disrespectful workplaces are at greater risk for losing key talent. When employees leave an organization on their own, they are often the employees with the most skills and potential. The reason for this is simple: they are the ones who are desired by other companies and, therefore, have more employment options. Based on years of conversations with human resource professionals, in disrespectful work environments, it is clear that there is little intrinsic motivation for these employees to stay when they can likely make the same amount of money working for a company where employees are treated better.

> In 2002, Captain D. Michael Abrashoff published his New York Times Bestseller, *It's Your Ship – Management Techniques From the Best Damn Ship in the Navy.* In his book he described the results of an internal study by the U.S. Armed Forces to determine why so many service men and women were not re-enlisting after their original tours of duty. He wrote:

"Pondering all of this in the context of my post as the new captain of Ben fold, I read some exit surveys, interviews conducted by the military to find out why people are leaving. I assumed that low pay would be the first, but in fact, it was fifth. The top reason was not being treated with respect or dignity; second was being prevented from making an impact on the organization; third, not being listened to; and forth, not being rewarded with more responsibility. Talk about an eye-opener."[1]

Poor communication patterns and practices.

While not a technical description, communication patterns within organizations that tolerate disrespectful behavior can become constipated. Information gets plugged up and frequently does not get shared as quickly and widely as it should. The rationale is, in the presence of the negative emotions mentioned previously, people's motivation for how and what they communicate with others becomes skewed. Rather than sharing thoughts, opinions and data to make sure everyone has the best information, the process becomes more calculated. People selectively share, or withhold, information based on what they perceive will make them look good, create an advantage over others or keep them out of trouble.

Lower client satisfaction and higher customer turnover.

Any organization that tolerates disrespectful behaviors in operations involving customer interaction faces the risk of alienating their client base. This is true whether the industry is manufacturing, healthcare, insurance or retail. People generally do a poor job at isolating emotions. If an employee feels they have been treated with disrespect by a co-worker or supervisor, it is likely to impact their interactions with people who have no connection to the disrespectful behaviors. It will show up as complaining, a lack of patience or possibly a general unwillingness to give the extra effort required to solve a problem. In certain industries, such as healthcare, this may even affect critical outcome measures.

Lower employee productivity.

While disrespect comes in many forms, it almost always damages performance. This is true at the individual level and often migrates to the group level. The primary reason is that it takes energy to respond and protect ourselves from disrespectful behaviors. Every time our brain has to divert its attention and energy to manage disrespectful elements within the environment, it represents a lost opportunity for the hiring organization. The brain taps its store of glucose to protect itself from danger rather than problem-solving.

The disrespect doesn't have to be overt or intentional. A colleague once shared his perspective of what it was like to be gay in an organization that did not openly have a policy of inclusion for the LGBT members of its workforce. What this meant for him was that every day he came to work, he had to spend a significant part of his energy simply trying to maintain the illusion that he was like everyone else. When people talked about what they did with their families over the weekend, he would either intentionally avoid participation in these conversations or use very guarded language that would not give away the fact that he was gay. If pressed for details, he would sometimes make things up just so he would appear to fit in with those who were straight. He had to spend additional energy making sure that what he shared on that day didn't contradict anything he might have said previously. It was an exhausting way to go through each day for five years. Think of the energy lost that could have been spent productively working!

Poor ability to respond to changes in their competitive environment.

As previously noted, the human brain only has so much energy to spend each day. Every molecule of glucose our brains have to spend protecting and defending ourselves in disrespectful environments represents energy that can't be spent on value-creating work. This includes monitoring and planning how to stay ahead of our competition, thinking about how to integrate new technology and making sure that our customers are satisfied and thrilled to have their needs taken care of by us. Disrespect simply becomes a distraction and energy drain on the entire organization.

What Happens When the Leader Is the Problem?

One of the greatest challenges in working with client organizations is that senior leaders and top managers often are blind to their personal role in the dysfunctional symptoms that they hire companies like mine to help resolve. In 2011, our company was retained to help with the training and development of the mid-level managers for a 400+ person engineering department in a well-known consumer products company. As part of our effort, we implemented a 360° feedback process for everyone who was in a leadership role within the group. The purpose was to help them better understand the perceptions that were driving employee attitudes within their department. It was very successful.....with one exception.

The most senior member of the team, the VP of Engineering, did not complete the 360° process. At first, this was attributed to a heavy task load and busy travel schedule. Upon further investigation, and multiple second chances to participate, a different reality became apparent. This individual intentionally chose not to participate. When questioned directly, he hemmed and hawed and came up with multiple reasons why it wasn't as important for him to complete the process as it was for his staff. In hindsight, I think he may actually have believed some of his own excuses, but to an outsider, and more importantly to his own staff, it was apparent that he simply was not willing to make himself open to feedback. Sadly, comments and insights gleaned from others in the organization squarely pointed to this key player as the source of much conflict, animosity and confusion, both within and outside his group. His disrespectful behaviors included publicly criticizing those who reported directly to him and talking behind the backs of those at his own level, earning him the reputation of being a back stabber.

As often happens, this VP resigned "to pursue new opportunities" with another organization. Miraculously, not only did the morale improve within the group, but so did the group's performance and stature within the company. While this was an obvious case of addition by subtraction for both the department and organization, I couldn't help wondering where this individual landed next and what damage he might be causing. I wonder what would have happened if he had made himself open to feedback and been willing to do the hard work required to address some of his shortcomings.

Why do we treat each other with disrespect?

A basic question to ask at this point is why do people treat each other with disrespect? Is it based in selfishness? Does it come from our disregard for the well-being of others? Does it come from ignorance? Or, could it possibly come from low self-esteem? It may be some or all of these reasons depending on the situation. One point is clear: the path toward disrespect is far easier and more convenient than the path toward respect. It takes very little evidence to justify on the front end and can usually be rationalized after the fact by selectively tying it to less-than-perfect behavior of others.

Psychopaths among us

Based on a scale created by psychologist Robert Hare, anywhere from 1-2% of the general population could be categorized as psychopathic. By definition, this means that they demonstrate a pervasive pattern of showing disregard for, and violating the rights of, others. Because the origins of psychopathic tendencies may be biological in nature and genetically predisposed, there may not be a lot that others can do to change or influence the behavior of psychopaths. It is crucial that individuals who fit this profile not be promoted to senior levels of leadership. As history has shown, psychopaths can be extremely successful in pursuing their goals. They also leave a wake of human destruction that ends up causing severe and sometimes permanent damage to their organizations. Some of the personalities involved with the colossal implosion of Enron make this abundantly clear.

Neuroscientists estimate that a similar percentage of people are physiologically immune to the effects of the oxytocin molecule. This naturally occurring compound is produced by most mammals, and is credited with creating emotional bonds between people. The release of oxytocin can be triggered in mothers by nursing infants, by intimate contact between couples, or simply by hugs, warm smiles and friendly interactions. Multiple studies have shown that the presence of oxytocin increases the degree of trust that people have in those with whom they are interacting. In his extraordinarily popular YouTube video, University of Santa Clara psychologist Dr. Paul Zak famously refers to the small percentage of people immune to the effects of oxytocin by a non-technical designation. He said, "We called them bastards."

Selfishness and self-interest

Let's face it; we have all behaved selfishly at one time or another. In part, this capacity is genetically wired into the human DNA as an element of our survival in a world with historically limited resources. In past generations, and currently in many parts of the world, the acquisition of food or other material privilege for one person, at the expense of another, meant a better chance of long-term survival for them and their offspring.

It was only when our species adopted more advanced, tribal characteristics that we began to demonstrate behaviors that perpetuated group survival. Somehow, our brains made the connection that some degree of "we" had a better chance of survival than "me." This complex evolutionarily insight was the origin of the first *social contracts* and the behaviors we now link to exchange theory. Fast forward to modern times and our brains operate on the same instinctive instruction set.

> *"Good leaders make people feel that they're at the very heart of things, not at the periphery."*
>
> —Warren G. Bennis

As it pertains to how we treat others, our brains are constantly calculating our interaction strategies with others, executed in fractions of a second, based upon the imagined outcomes and "rewards" for specific behaviors. When we perceive ourselves to be at a deficit in some way, especially with elements related to physical survival or social acceptance/recognition, it potentially makes it more difficult to engage others in a way that gives respect unless we can link it to our own future rewards. Although not particularly flattering, it is in our nature to calculate the future value of treating others with respect!

Given this predisposition toward self-interest, the questions we have to consciously challenge ourselves with each day are:

- What is the behavioral path related to my treatment of others that will lead to the greatest future rewards, both for me individually and "us" together?

- How wide of a net can I spread for my definition of "us" – my family, my community, my department, my company, all human beings?

- Am I willing to spend my individual time and effort today, requiring the expenditure of somewhat finite physical energy, for a potentially more prosperous and rewarding tomorrow?

Without getting too deep into the psychological discussion of altruism and our capacity for delayed gratification, it is safe to conclude that any argument for respectful behavior of others presupposes that we can overcome more instinctual urges to satisfy our own wants and needs first. If we can see no benefit to treating others with respect, then we won't, at least not with any consistency.

We Don't Know What We Don't Know

We can't fix what we don't know is broken, and unfortunately for most of us, that includes our scope of awareness. While broken may be a harsh term, few of us will attain the degree of awareness about others required to fully treat them with respect. As the saying goes, "We go with the horse that brung us." The information we rely on in our interactions with others is based on a combination of reference points amassed over the years. In what Robert Burton, M.D., referred to as "the hidden layer,"[8] our brains create a unique blueprint of how we see the world, those around us and ourselves.

This blueprint was in part inherited, dictated to us and pieced together over time based on our unique interpretation of past experiences. Despite its subjective nature, it represents our truth and reality at any point in time. When we interact with others, we're not so much interacting with them as they really are, but with the data we have pieced together over time about them or people like them (race, gender, age, etc.). This information tends to be persistent. Even though we can update our mental "software," our brains find it easier to reuse what we already have. So we try to force new people and situations into old patterns rather than creating fresh, more appropriate, patterns. Although this approach takes less energy, it also bears the potential seeds of disrespect. The perceptions we have of other people are rarely completely accurate.

The human brain is a magnificent piece of work. It perceives new information at lightning quick speed and instantaneously compares it to thousands of past reference points and patterns to come up with the best matches. When we meet new people, in a split second we access multiple reference points that tell us about people "like them." This includes the vast spectrum of information known as stereotypes, which is defined as standardized mental pictures/models that we create for members of different groups. They can be for groups as large as "male" or as small as "trombone players." No matter what the group, most of us are able to piece together some rudimentary description of the people that belong to this group. Contrary to what many people believe, stereotypes are not bad. They are simply tools that the brain uses to efficiently categorize new reference points as quickly as possible. If it weren't for stereotypes, the amount of time and mental effort it would take us to figure out how to interact with people would make ordinary social interactions impossible. Our brains would be so busy assessing and categorizing the new data that we wouldn't have time for anything else.

As helpful as stereotypes are, they have significant and obvious limitations. Stereotypes are oversimplified pictures of the groups they describe. By their very nature, they allow no room for variation and are easily reinforced by only fragments of supporting evidence. Stereotypes reside in our minds as truths until

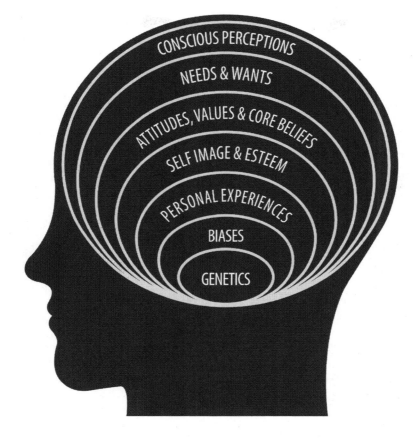

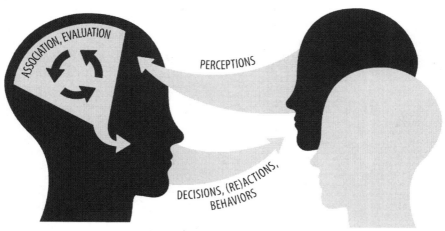

displaced by new information. The only way to verify the degree to which a stereotype applies to people we associate with is through direct, one-on-one engagement.

Stereotypes by themselves would be relatively harmless except for one problem. We interact with others and take action based on stereotypes as if they were indisputable facts. In the absence of first-hand data, it's all we have to go on and so we do. When we interact with people as though they are the sum of stereotypes that we've assigned to them, we are assured of being disrespectful in our approach. This mental process is the genesis of prejudice.

There are situations where prejudicial behavior may not be damaging to the person to which it is directed, but can instead be damaging to others. An example of this is when we meet someone who we associate with a group that we have assigned favorable stereotypes such as above-average intelligence, athleticism, particular skills or abilities. A person who graduated from an Ivy League university may be shown a preference over someone who graduated from a community college. Stereotypes often have a kernel of truth, but who's to say whether that actually makes the individual from an Ivy League university a better hire or more intelligent. The result is that a person may be shown favoritism even though it is unearned. This type of *micro-inequity* is common and frequently interpreted as a subtle sign of disrespect.

PART

II

"To laugh often and much; to win the respect of intelligent people and the affection of children; to earn the appreciation of honest critics and to endure the betrayal of false friends; to appreciate beauty; to find the best in others; to leave the world a bit better whether by a healthy child, a garden patch or a redeemed social condition; to know even one life has breathed easier because you have lived. This is to have succeeded"

~ Ralph Waldo Emerson

Tools for Building Respectful Work Cultures

The Gift of Feedback

A commitment to a respectful workplace becomes part of the fabric of an organization's culture. The greatest leverage to shape and influence culture is at the top of an organization. Individual contributors, supervisors and mid-level managers pay careful attention to how their senior leaders act and behave. Then, depending on their own aspirations, one of two things happens. They either try to emulate the attitudes and behaviors they think will lead to their own success or they distance themselves from the leaders they don't respect or whose behaviors they view as counterproductive. Either way, those at the top of the organization are always under the microscope. Because of this, having a clear and accurate perception of how we are viewed by others is extraordinarily important. To attempt to lead others without this vantage point is, at best, a quick road to mediocrity. At worst, it is a recipe for disaster.

One of the easiest ways to understand how we are perceived by others is to participate in a 360° feedback process. This process reveals perspectives from all levels of the organizations – from above, from peers and from those who report to us. As long as

the 360° feedback process is administered by skilled practitioners and used only for feedback (never for performance reviews),
these instruments can provide valuable feedback that helps leaders and managers better understand how they impact the performance of those around them. While there are many solid 360°
tools available, what's most important is that the tool selected
captures the emotional impact that leaders and managers have
on those around them. Do they treat people in ways that increase
their commitment to the organization and build their capabilities, or do they alienate them and diminish their long-term
potential?

> *"All meaningful and lasting change starts on the
> inside and works its way out."*
>
> —Bob Moawad

Getting the commitment from some leaders to participate in a
360° feedback process is difficult. It amazes me how many
senior leaders come up with excuses why they can't participate.
Some claim it is a waste of time; that it's not important what
their subordinates think. Others say they already know what people around them think, so they don't need a survey. In most
cases, this type of resistance can be interpreted as a sign of fear-
fulness and vulnerability. These emotions are understandable;
the first step is the scariest. The reward for opening ourselves up
to honest feedback from our peers is priceless in its value to our
future success.

The Power of Humility

In the fall of 2011, "Tom", CEO of one of the world's
most successful restaurant chains in the past 50 years,

set in motion a leadership development initiative that had the impact of supercharging his entire 250-person leadership team. Having recently returned to actively leading the company he founded years earlier, he connected with his leaders in a way that was both courageous and meaningful. For the first time in his career, Tom participated in his own 360° feedback process and received candid feedback from 11 others within the organization about his behaviors, leadership style and feelings that they had about him as their leader.

Opening ourselves up to this level of feedback, at least initially, is an act of courage. It's courageous because it brings all our observable flaws into the open and makes us exceptionally vulnerable. It is this vulnerability, ironically, that has the potential to make a strong leader even stronger.

The feedback Tom received from his team was similar to what would be expected from other senior leaders. There were some things he did very well and others that needed work. This might be the end of the story, but for one exception. Most 360° participants share their results only with their own bosses and maybe an executive coach. They then create an action plan that tries to leverage their strengths and improve in the areas needed. In some cases, they may share their action plans with those who provided them feedback. Tom did something quite different. He publicly shared his results with the top 250 leaders who were being tasked with helping to transform the chain and prepare it for success in the upcoming decade.

This public display of candor and humility was one of the greatest demonstrations of respect for his managers that a senior leader in his position could have offered. The respect and trust that it showed he had for those who reported to him, as one observer noted, "Literally set the group on fire." Courage led to vulnerability, which was interpreted as humility. Humility then bred trust, communicated profound respect and significantly boosted engagement.

Most importantly, all of the company's stakeholders have benefitted from this seemingly simple act. Customers are happy, as reflected by revenue growth,

employee engagement scores are up and stockholders have been rewarded handsomely with a 65% increase in the share price of their stock in the six months following.

The Power of Trust

One of the most important assets created by respectful leaders is trust. Trust leads to the perception of safety and the feeling of safety helps free organizational potential. Even when the environment outside an organization may be in flux from the economy, competition or changing technology, trust that co-workers and leaders will look out for each other's best interest and be truthful creates a type of stability that will endure outside pressures.

> *"A man who doesn't trust himself can never really trust anyone else."*
>
> —Jean Francois Paul De Gondi, Cardinal De Retz

The simplest way to create trust is to pursue an unconditional policy of doing the "right thing" at every level within the organization. Although this is a simple concept, it is often difficult to implement because doing the "right thing" may require us to subordinate what's in our individual best interest. Consider the following real-world example:

In November, 2008 the U.S. and much of the world was still at the front end of what would prove to be the greatest and most prolonged recession since the

Great Depression. While few industries were unaffected, manufacturing was hit disproportionately hard. With layoffs at record levels, consumers' appetite for durable goods dried up to a mere trickle. This not only affected direct manufacturers of consumer products, but also most of their tier one and tier two suppliers. One such company was Metaullics Systems in Solon, Ohio, a division of Pyrotek, Incorporated. Metaullics Systems manufactured high-end mixing and pumping equipment for molten aluminum, and its products were used all over the world.

The recession hit Metaullics hard. With their revenue off by nearly 60%, they were forced to make deep cuts to their staffing levels. It was how this process was implemented that allowed the company to boost morale and commitment while increasing per/employee productivity. Rich Henderson, the plant's Operations Manager, followed a policy of complete transparency with the company's employees. Revenue, customer orders, backorders and inventory turn information were all regularly shared at the company's town hall meetings. Even in difficult times, he followed this policy religiously.

When the company's orders fell from $1.6 million to $610,000 per month, Henderson remained candid with his employees. It was an extremely difficult time, and painful cuts were necessary. The way they were handled would be, in part, determined by the employees. While the employees at Metaullics had recently decertified their union, it was their decision to continue following union guidelines for layoffs. Any terminations would be made only after contractors were first let go. An offer was made to bridge any employees who were close to retirement. By the time the cuts were complete, almost 40% of the company's employees had

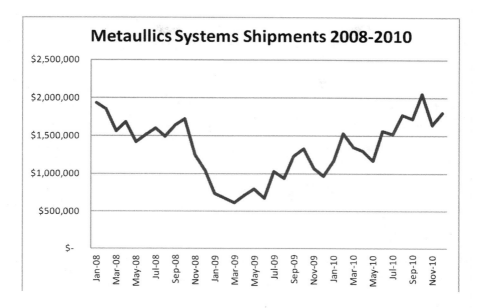

lost their jobs. The number would have been higher except that several employees offered to initiate cuts in their own compensation to save some of their colleagues' jobs.

To an outside observer, what was astounding was the degree of loyalty, trust and enthusiasm that resulted from Henderson's candor during bleak economic times. Despite orders dropping lower each month, Metaullics' employees didn't act as though their fate was in anyone's hands but their own. When there were no client orders to work on, they found other things to do. They cleaned the plant. They tackled any small repairs they could find. They caulked windows and painted walls. They did everything they could to stay productive and make the business better prepared and more efficient when the anticipated recovery arrived.

As with most businesses, the recovery finally found its way to Metaullics. Not only did the company regain its original level of client orders, but it actually grew them over 20% and did it with 10% fewer employees. Just as importantly, it emerged with the enthusiasm, hope and commitment of its most valuable employees intact.

How do you cultivate trust in organizations? As with most worthy pursuits, building trust isn't easy. The first step involves a shift in agendas by senior leaders. In alignment with traditional organization models, most leaders and senior managers see themselves at the top of their respective organizational hierarchies. By design, it is presumed that their jobs are to develop objectives and map out strategies for growing the business. Even if not stated, the implication is that everyone else is there to support the leader's agenda and help execute the resulting plans. Employees are tools, sometimes affectionately referred to as human assets, to be utilized as efficiently as possible.

Organizational cultures that emerge under this human asset model don't typically develop high levels of organic trust. On the scale of priorities, employees are secondary to business goals. To grow trust, managers and leaders need to flip this model on its head and put the success and well-being of their employees squarely in the middle of their business agendas. Structurally, this is sometimes referred to as the servant leadership model,[9] where leaders are at the bottom of their organizational hierarchies. When this happens, manager and leader behaviors change because their motivations change. Successfully adopting and supporting the agendas of those below them become part of the metrics by which the leaders are evaluated.

Trust Made Simple

During a recent workshop for the sales and marketing leadership team of a Fortune 50 chemical company, one senior leader shared a story about trust that he attributed to one of his former bosses. In his words, the man conducted his life by simple and powerful values. When it came to how to lead others, only two questions needed to be answered:

1. Would your mother be proud?

2. How would you feel if someone were to ask your son or daughter to do the same thing?

Respect through osmosis

In a workforce that increasingly reflects the demographic differences within the population, getting people from dissimilar age, gender and ethnic backgrounds to work together collaboratively can be a real challenge. When you add differences in core values, moral codes and political leanings, it can prove to be almost impossible. While most people intellectually "get" that diversity of ideas and opinions should lead to more creative approaches and solutions, pervasive stereotypes and the lack of familiarity and trust can create emotional roadblocks that inhibit true synergistic thinking. Until team members make the effort to work through their differences and discover their similarities, the required element of trust will remain elusive. What's a manager to do?

Fortunately, the fields of psychology and organizational development can provide insight. Specifically, the principal of *contact hypothesis* holds that people who are fundamentally different from each other in significant ways (race, age, social values, etc.) can work through prejudices and be coaxed into working together collaboratively under the right conditions. This can even be accomplished if the differences have led to a state of conflict. The most important factors for this principle to work are:

- All substantial sources of conflict be dealt with or removed;

- All individuals have equal power, stature and privileges;

- The members of the overall group be given a task which can't be accomplished successfully unless all members work together (structured interdependence); and

- The environment in which the "contact" takes place is neutral and conducive to positive, friendly interactions.

Ideally, contact hypothesis leads to higher levels of group productivity and the dilution of negative stereotypes that different members may have of each others' groups.

12 Rules of Respect

As previously mentioned, respect is demonstrated in different ways and practiced one interaction at a time. These 12 Rules of Respect illustrate ways of thinking and behaving around others. They have been shown to be tremendously powerful at positively affecting how people perceive both others and themselves when interacting.

1. Be aware of your nonverbal and extra verbal cues.

Whenever we are interacting in person with others, we are deploying and responding to multiple modes of communication. First, there are the words themselves. Language is a tool of nuance and using the right words to create the desired meaning can be an important skill that we learn over the course of our lives. Even more critical than the actual words are the countless nonverbal and extra verbal cues we employ to deliver the words. The simple phrase, "We should probably talk about this," can mean any number of things depending on how it is said.

Psychologist Albert Mehrabian is often quoted for suggesting that as much as 93% of the messaging that occurs between individuals when talking in person transpires through nonverbal and extra verbal cues. This is not to suggest that words are inconsequential, but rather that the interpretation of our true intent is more accurately determined by the way in which our words are delivered. Extra verbal cues include the speed with which we speak, our volume relative to background noise and others, our inflection and our willingness to pause to make space for others to speak. Nonverbal cues can be subtle, such as physical proximity to those with whom we speak. Obvious nonverbal cues can include hand gestures, eye movement and facial expressions. It is important to remember that when our nonverbal and extra verbal cues appear to convey a different message than our words, the human brain is programmed to give more credence to the nonverbal.

> *"We often refuse to accept an idea merely because of the tone of voice in which it has been expressed is unsympathetic to us."*
>
> —Friedrich Nietzsche

If we're trying to communicate respect, it's critical that we minimize the occurrence of cues that suggest otherwise. Behaviors such as yelling, rolling our eyes, shaking our head in opposition, interrupting, sighing, avoiding eye contact, frowning and foot tapping can't be ignored, no matter how respectful our actual words may be. That is why it is a critical skill to synchronize all of our communication modes to deliver the same message.

Technology plays an increasing role in contributing to misunderstandings between people, including the unintended perception of disrespect. Despite the benefits we derive from e-mailing, texting, posting and tweeting, there is a dark side. When we strip away the accompanying delivery cues that human beings have evolved to notice, our electronically delivered words can take on a life of their own. Because *intended* meaning can easily be trumped by *assumed* meaning, it is best to utilize face-to-face communication whenever the subject or message has the potential of evoking emotions. When in person communication isn't possible, a phone call is the next best option.

2. Develop curiosity for the perspectives of others.

Like many people, I woke up this morning knowing exactly how the world was – at least according to me. I knew which faith was the right faith, which political party can successfully lead our country into the future and what social values were best for America. That's my story and I'm sticking to it! Okay, not exactly, but you get the point. As each of us navigates our way through the twists and turns of life, love and business, we do so from our unique perspectives. What we usually don't do, however, is explore the perspectives of others, even when they're on similar journeys.

> *"Most of the successful people I've known are the ones who do more listening than talking."*
>
> —Bernard M. Baruch

Empathy, defined as the ability to understand the emotional position of others, starts with curiosity and is demonstrated through active inquiry.

- "I wonder how Adam might feel about that."

- "I wonder what made Sue respond that way."

- "How is Carl likely to respond when I share my idea?"

- "I wonder what I could do to make Tamika feel better."

Sometimes we silently ask ourselves the questions. Other times we speak out loud to those in our presence. Either way, empathy is demonstrated when it becomes evident to others around us that we are interested in what they think, why they think it and how they feel about it. When this happens, it becomes easier to communicate respect to others, even if we disagree with them.

3. Assume that everyone is smart about something.

While assumptions can sometimes get us into trouble, there is one that usually doesn't. Whenever I'm meeting someone for the first time, or even a new group of people, I like to assume that each one of them is intelligent in their own way. Because I like to think I'm smart, it is reasonable to assume that other people like to think they also are smart. The only difference is that we all got smart through different histories and life experiences.

My story is unique to me. I grew up in a suburb of Columbus, Ohio. I went to parochial schools and then on to graduate from The Ohio State University. While at OSU, I interned with two well-known companies and joined one as a full-time employee after graduation. From there, I moved to Colorado and then Oregon before settling in the Cleveland, Ohio area. Along the way, I earned an MBA and, in 1997, left the safe cubicles of a Fortune 50 company to start my own business. Although there are undoubtedly other people in the world who grew up in Columbus, moved out of state, moved back to Ohio and started their own company, the pool is getting smaller and the nuances greater.

Since 1997, I've worked on five continents and presented my ideas to over a quarter million business leaders and professionals. Because of this unique journey, I became fairly smart in my particular fields of expertise. This does not make me smarter than others around me, just smart in a different way. That's the way it is with most people. Others that we meet are smart, only their stories are different, and they got smart through different life experiences. What about you? How did you get smart? More importantly, how does it feel when the people you work with treat you as if you are smart?

4. Become a better listener by shaking your "but"!

Words are tools of nuance. They are not good or bad; they are merely tools, and knowing which words to use and not to use in a conversation can make a big difference. One word in particular can be used in a way that hinders our ability to show respect. That word is "but." While it's difficult to imagine any conversation of length not using this word, when and how we use it has a tremendous impact in communicating whether or not we value someone's opinion and ideas.

Coming from a large family, I'm familiar with the "yah, but" phenomenon. It goes something like this: You're having a conversation with someone, typically about a subject that both of you have different opinions about, like whose turn it is to host Thanksgiving dinner this year. When one person gets halfway through explaining his or her position, the other jumps in with a "yah, but…" and commandeers the metaphorical microphone. Then mid-stream through his or her point, the courtesy is returned. After several minutes, instead of having a productive exchange of ideas and opinions, both sides are battling to have their perspective accepted and neither party feels heard. Similar incidents take place at work, with different subjects and power dynamics.

While interrupting others is disrespectful on its own, the language that follows can make it worse. The danger with using the word "but" when discussing different ideas and perspectives is that it negates whatever came before it. As soon as your idea or opinion is presented, a "but" from someone else has the psychological impact of saying, "You're wrong." The word "however" is no better. While possibly sounding a bit politer, it subtlety communicates the same lack of regard for what came before it. To better understand the dynamics of the word "but," consider the following exchange:

> Bill: "John, my team has kicked this around for over a week. As a company, we've got to do a better job distinguishing ourselves from our competitors. If we…"

> John: "Yah, but the only way to do that is to spend more money on advertising and we just don't have that in the budget right now."

> Bill: "But, John, listen, there's more than one way to do this. Does advertising cost money? Sure it does, but…"

> John: "No buts, John. The budget has been set for over six months and we're not going to change it."

While this conversation can continue, the tone has already been set. Rather than sharing their ideas and perspectives, John and Bill are battling over their ideas. Little information is being shared, and both feel frustrated. If John happens to be Bill's boss, more than likely Bill feels devalued. If others were present when this exchange took place, Bill also feels embarrassed. Because of the subtle disrespect shown, the team has made no progress in solving the challenge it faces. More significantly, rather than continuing to think about ideas to address the situation, Bill has been temporarily sidelined while he deals with the emotional impact of having been treated with disrespect.

Let's rewind the exchange, eliminate the interruptions and try to change a few of the words.

> Bill: "John, my team has discussed this for over a week. As a company, we've got to do a better job distinguishing ourselves from our competitors. If we can create a higher level of visibility in our key markets and position ourselves as *the* supplier of choice, I think we can hit, and maybe event beat, or Q4 sales forecast."

> John: "Bill, *I hear what you're saying and it makes a lot of sense.* A higher level of visibility within markets like Chicago and D.C. could make a huge difference for us. *At the same time,* won't we have to spend more money on advertising? All of the directors, including me, are under a lot of pressure to watch budgets right now."

> Bill: "*You're right, John,* advertising does cost money. *And, I hear you loud and clear* about the budget. There has been lots of gossip in the halls about belt-tightening, so I've already been thinking about ways

around this challenge. What if we scaled back on our trade show budget and reallocated some of that money to advertising? Some of our clients are tightening their belts also and many aren't even going to the shows this year. They still read the trade journals and they still listen to the radio."

John: "You know, Bill, *I'd never thought about that*. I think *you might be on to something* with the shows. And with some of our competitors also scaling back budgets, I'll bet we might even be able to get ad space at a discount next quarter."

Look at the difference a few words can make. Simply by not interrupting and replacing the "buts" with words that validate and convey consideration, the entire tone changed. Without asking for it, both Bill and John received something they valued tremendously: validation. Bill got validation that his ideas were carefully thought out, and John received validation that his budget concerns were not discounted. By working together they made significant progress on their challenge and remained fully engaged in finding the best path forward. If we want to have a productive exchange of ideas in a respectful manner, then it becomes crucial that we demonstrate value for each others' positions.

> "I know that you believe you understand what you think I said, but I'm not sure you realize that what you heard is not what I meant."
>
> —Friedrich Nietzsche

5. Look for opportunities to connect with and support others.

Differences of opinion and occasional conflicts are inevitable, woven tightly into the fabric of the human social experience.

81

Sometimes the source of these conflicts is clear and readily understood, as in competitions, and other times they just happen because orbits collide without warning. Such was the case my junior year in college when I was a Resident Advisor. My first RA assignment was to serve as the resource for a group of 60 guys living in three separate wings of the dormitory. My group included a high percentage of scholarship athletes, mostly freshmen, and this was their first time living on their own. There were 12 football players, four basketball players and two golfers on the floors. Athletes living in college dorms at an NCAA Division I school have different experiences from non-athlete students, including dissimilar schedules, access to resources, separate eating facilities and their own "in group" behavior norms. Add a few contraband beers into the mix on weekends and you have an interesting recipe.

One Saturday evening shortly after the end of football season, I was making rounds when Jamie H., the lone junior football player on the floor, suddenly crashed through the double doors I was about to go through, nearly knocking me into a wall. Jamie was about 6'2", 220 lbs. and built like a freight train. The first thing I realized was that he was extremely agitated, had been drinking and was in absolutely no mood to be messed with. "Whoa, whoa, whoa," I said, trying to defuse his anger. "Get out of my way and mind your own business," he shouted. Clearly I was in the wrong place at the wrong time. I didn't want a physical confrontation; that would not have ended well for me, but I also didn't want Jamie to take his anger out on any of the other guys on the floor.

Primarily, out of a sense of self-preservation, I blurted out, "Jamie, I'm not sure what happened to you tonight; is there anything I can do to help?" Of all the things I could have said, that evidently was the right choice. Almost immediately, his demeanor changed. Jamie stepped back, took a deep breath and apologized. "Sorry man," he said. "It's got nothin' to do with you." I looked at him with the most empathic look I could conjure up and continued. "Seriously, is there anything I can do to help?" At that point, the confrontation was over. Jamie actually smiled and said, "Nah, I'll be alright. Sorry 'bout that." He shyly looked down and went back the way he came.

While I never did figure out what Jamie was upset about, I accidentally learned a valuable lesson. Even in the heat of conflict, there are ways to connect with people if we want to. When we demonstrate a willingness to move away from our immediate agenda and search for positions of agreement first, it makes working through the actual differences a bit easier.

"The self is not something ready-made but something in continuous formation through choice of action."

—John Dewey

When it comes to connecting with others, one of the greatest skills we can develop is the ability to use language that lets people know it is safe for them to be their complete selves in our presence. This requires two things. First, we don't assume everyone is like us, even if they look like us. Second, it is genuinely okay for people to be their *complete* selves around us, regardless of the differences between us. Assuming these criteria are met, we often need to explicitly use language that reflects this. For example, if I have a devout belief in a particular religion, do I use language around others that lets them know that I hold them in high regard even if they don't share my beliefs? If I'm heterosexual with pictures of my wife and children displayed in my office, do I use language that informs my LGBT co-workers or subordinates, whose sexual orientation may be unknown to me, that it's okay for them to be different? We benefit ourselves, others and our organization when we cultivate a vocabulary that lets people know that, despite our differences, there are likely many more similarities between us.

6. Explain why you disagree, when you do.

On January 28, 1986, one of the greatest space disasters in history took place in the skies off the coast of Central Florida. The space shuttle Challenger exploded 73 seconds after liftoff, taking the lives of all seven crew members. In the months that followed, what made this disaster worse was news that it could have been prevented. An internal investigation revealed that Challenger was launched that morning at a temperature lower than was approved for the O-ring seals on the shuttle booster rockets. More troubling was that several NASA engineers were aware of this before the launch and never voiced their concerns at a level that could have stopped the launch.

The drawn-out investigation revealed no malice on the part of the engineers. Rather, it discovered serious problems within NASA's culture. People were afraid to speak their mind, especially when their opinions might contradict those of their superiors. The decision to launch that morning was made at the highest levels within NASA, and nobody below wanted to stick their neck out and say, "Wait this may not be safe." The rest is history.

It is disrespectful when we fail to share our observations and opinions in order to avoid conflict. We have an obligation to others to be truthful with our perspectives and points of view. When done with civility, tact and room for counter arguments, sharing our perspectives leads to the best decisions and optimal results. It also prevents the accumulation of "baggage" that builds up when we keep things bottled up.

The one caveat is that sharing perspectives has to go both ways. We have an obligation to share our perspectives and opinions with others, especially when the safety or other important outcomes are involved. We also have an obligation to be good listeners. Even when we haven't asked for the opinions of others, we must demonstrate some faith in their good intentions when they do.

7. Admit where you need to personally grow, stretch or change.

It is safe to say that most of us go through life critiquing other people's actions and decisions based on our own perspectives and standards. When relationships become strained or our opinions of others become overly critical, we typically take the position that it's other people who are doing something wrong. It takes less effort to think this way, because it places the onus for improvement and change on others. As convenient (and efficient) as this may be for our brains, it can easily become an excuse for not engaging in the learning, "flexing" and personal growth that should be pursued by us.

An example is the dynamic in the relationship that forms between husbands and wives, partners or significant others. The longer we are together, the more established our patterns of interaction become and the blinder we become to our own deficiencies. After five years of marriage, my wife Kim gradually began pointing out to me that I had a hard time being wrong about things. My original reaction was to resist this notion and adopt the position that I usually was right! If I could rationalize and articulate why my point of view made more sense than hers, then I must be correct. As you can imagine, this kind of logic grew tiring for my wife. It would be difficult to stay married or in a relationship where your partner made you feel that you were always wrong. I'm happy to report that, despite my bad habits, we've been married almost 15 years. One of the reasons my wife still puts up with me is that I've gotten better at acknowledging my own flaws, which I realize are many, and am willing to work on them.

> *"Change will never happen when people lack the ability and courage to see themselves for who they are."*
>
> —Bryant H. McGill

As we develop the desire and the willingness to hold ourselves up to the proverbial "bright light" for an occasional reality check, two things happen. First, we become infinitely easier to be around because we are less critical of others. Second, we grow in wisdom and perspective. That's because we start considering that, in situations where we might initially view others critically, the issues may be ours to deal with and not theirs.

8. Learn to be wrong on occasion.

My favorite of the 12 rules, and the one hardest to follow, is to learn to be wrong. Neurologist and author Robert Burton, M.D., artfully captured this sentiment when he reflected on the pioneering research conducted by social psychologists James Carlsmith and Leon Festinger on the topic of cognitive dissonance:

"Festinger's seminal observation: The more committed we are to a belief, the harder it is to relinquish, even in the face of overwhelming contradictory evidence. Instead of acknowledging error in judgment and abandoning the opinion, we tend to develop a new attitude or belief that will justify retaining it."

Little did my wife know that it wasn't just me. Indeed, as a species, it appears we are more prone to rationalize than be rational. Burton went on to write that, from a neurological perspective, there is absolutely no correlation between our degree of certainty about a subject and the likelihood that we are actually correct in our beliefs. This means that our feeling of certainty about something is nothing more than a strong emotion. The stronger the emotion, the more likely we are to develop blind spots around it. While unintentional, a mindset of certainty can also set the stage for potentially disrespectful treatment of others, especially toward those who do not share our closely-held beliefs.

"Let us be a little humble; let us think that the truth may not perhaps be entirely with us."

—Jawaharial Nehru

A demonstration of our propensity to rationalize is when faith and fact collide. Think about it. We all have those hot-button topics; the ones in which our positions become emotionally entrenched and any evidence to the contrary is discounted before it's even considered. What subjects arouse strong feelings in you – your faith, political viewpoint, position on gay marriage or abortion? To what lengths would you go to try to get others to conform to or behave in accordance with the way you think?

An example that clearly illustrates this phenomenon is the discussion of gay rights and the nature of homosexuality in the United States. According to the 2009 Angus Reid Public Opinion survey, 47% of American adults believed that homosexuality is a lifestyle choice. By comparison, only 34% of those surveyed thought that it was something with which people were born.[10] What is interesting about these statistics is that available scientific data clearly and unequivocally paints a different picture. The research on the subject is so conclusive, that it is no longer considered a subject of debate in the scientific community. Homosexuality is no more a lifestyle choice than is heterosexuality. Nor is it a disease to be cured or a mental illness to be treated. To the contrary, the American Psychiatric Association has maintained the unambiguous position since 1973 that homosexuality is not a mental illness and warns against the dangers of trying to convert gays to being straight based upon moral or religious convictions. We still live in a society in which many are too willing to ignore hard data if it allows us to "be right" about our previously held convictions.

Being willing to consider other points of view, even when we "know" we are right, is a significant demonstration of respect to others. There's a greater benefit; we open the door to learning. When we genuinely consider points of view and data that run counter to what we believe to be true, only good things can happen. We demonstrate respect for others, increase our awareness of what they think and why they think that way, and alternately increase the likelihood that we will be able to work with them in a mutually productive manner. As American social author Eric Hoffer eloquently noted, "In times of change, learners inherit the earth, while the learned are beautifully equipped to deal with a world that no longer exists."

9. Never hesitate to say you are sorry.

If I had a nickel for every time I've said I'm sorry, I'd be rich. If I had a nickel for every time I should have said I'm sorry, I'd be retired. No one is perfect. Even if we are normally respectful in our interactions with others, we have those moments when we don't act our best, those moments that we wish we could erase and do over. Unfortunately, it is often when we're at our worst that our actions are most memorable to others. As previously mentioned, it's the way we're wired. Disrespectful behaviors that harm us are immediately sent to long-term memory where they are stored for future reference.

> *"A stiff apology is a second insult..... The injured party does not want to be compensated because he has been wronged; he wants to be healed because he has been hurt."*
>
> —G.K. Chesterton

Fortunately, we don't expect each other to be perfect. We do expect people to make it right when their words, actions or decisions cause damage. Yelling, misplaced blame, snide comments and public ridicule all create a chemical signature that is often repeatedly replayed in the minds of the receivers unless an honest apology is offered as close to the event as possible. If it isn't, the damage can worsen. The original incident often morphs into something much worse than it actually was. Remember, the human brain typically is not very good at remembering the exact details of events. We remember the emotions and, over time, recreate (sometimes invent) the emotions.

When the damage is done in public, to be effective the apology must occur in the same venue. This is due to the amplification that occurs whenever we publicly praise or criticize. Admittedly, this is sometimes easier said than done. Until we get in the habit of consistently holding ourselves accountable for how we treat others, saying that we're sorry in public demonstrates courage of the highest order. But, there is a reward for that courage. Publicly admitting that we've behaved poorly and expressing remorse for our actions displays vulnerability and humanness that actually makes us more effective leaders.

10. Intentionally engage others in ways that build their self-esteem.

We have all met people who have the ability to make us feel special. It is usually the result of many small things that they do. They ask questions and listen intently to our replies, smile and nod their head in approval when we share our ideas. They applaud our efforts and point out how the things we do make a difference. On occasion, they offer feedback in order to help us become more successful. What is it that guides some people to be better at this than others? It is intention, or at least it starts there. When we interact with others with the specific goal of building their sense of worth and confidence, we look for unique ways of doing so throughout the encounter.

Building esteem in people we work with or for requires a shift in agendas. It takes a shift in focus away from what we need to what others need. While possibly feeling counter-intuitive, it is the ability to make this shift that enables leaders and managers to become more influential and effective. So important is this capacity, that many practitioners in the field of leadership development believe it should be a baseline requirement for promotion to senior positions. Years ago, my colleague Teresa Welborne, Ph.D., President of eePulse, noted:

> "If you are in a leadership position and are not a people person, you become a liability to your organization. And if you're not willing to make the effort to become a people person, you should not be in a position of leadership."

Welborne's rationale is simple. If you're in a leadership position at any level within an organization, your number one job is to try to increase the capability and capacity of those who report to you. This focus is the surest and fastest way to improving the effectiveness of any team. Figuring out how to build each player's capacity is a one-on-one job and requires that we engage others in a manner that reflects what's important to them, not to us. As you make this investment in those who report to you, it builds trust, raises their confidence and reaffirms their long-term value to the organization. It also takes time and energy. If being a "people person" hasn't been a priority, making the initial change to focus on other people's agendas may be one that takes great effort.

11. Be respectful of time when making comments.

I hate to admit it - I've always been a talker. I was born that way. According to my parents, this behavior dominated my personality from about the time I was one year old. No matter what anybody else was talking about, my contributions needed to take center stage. It is even been rumored that my grandmother would on occasion tell me, "Paul Meshanko, there's a reason God gave you two ears and one mouth!" Now I personally find it hard to believe that my grandmother would ever have uttered those exact words to me, but it is possible.

> *"One of the most sincere forms of respect is actually listening to what another has to say."*
>
> —Bryant H. McGill

Learning to proportionally share our thoughts comes easier to some people. It requires a degree of social skill, awareness of our "position" relative to those we're speaking with and communication skills that allow us to tactfully make our points. More than these skills, the ability to interact consistently with others proportionally comes from our attitudinal predispositions toward them. Specifically, we need to continue to cultivate both curiosity and value for the perspectives of others. If we don't become curious or have value for what other people have to say, it is difficult to consistently fake the behaviors that demonstrate interest.

12. Smile!

Sometimes the most effective strategies are also the simplest. With rare exception, when we meet people who greet us with a smile, they are sending us important information about their intentions. If we return the smile, we do the same. When our brains detect strangers who are different from us, a smile is the universal nonverbal cue that our intentions are friendly. Extensive research shows that smiling shifts the mindset of the person displaying it. When we greet people with an intentional smile, even when that may not be our initial predisposition, we are actually less likely to harbor prejudicial or suspicious thoughts about them.[11] When it comes to respect, both giving and receiving smiles is pretty important.

> *"The shortest distance between two people is a smile."*
>
> —Anonymous

One word of caution: if you are not the type of person who has developed the reputation for smiling, be patient with its impact on those around you, especially those you don't know well. The brain tends to become suspicious when it detects abnormal behavior patterns from people that we already know. For example, if I were to go home and unexpectedly surprised my wife with flowers, I think her first response would be to ask me what I did or what I wanted! That notwithstanding, cultivating the habit of smiling when we meet people eventually pays considerable dividends to the quality of our relationships.

Changing Behavior Is the Key

As powerful as the 12 Rules of Respect can be, it would be unfair to proceed further without spending some time exploring the psychology and science of behavior change. We've all failed at changing our behaviors one time or another. Even when we've felt motivated to change the way we do things, old habits die hard. This phenomenon isn't the result of poor willpower or a lack of discipline or motivation. It is simply a matter of neural physiology. The behavior patterns we use the longest are the ones our brains are most skilled and efficient at using, even if they're not the ones we desire. This includes our interaction styles and patterns with other people. If I was a good listener yesterday, I'll probably be a good listener today and again tomorrow. If I habitually yelled when I got angry in the past, I most likely will yell in the future. Either way, these are the pathways our brains have gotten very good at flexing. Every time we flex an existing neural pathway, we make it stronger.

The adult human brain weighs about 4½ pounds and is comprised of approximately 100 billion neurons. Each of those neurons can be connected to 10,000 other neurons in an intricate network of synaptic pathways. Think of it as an extraordinarily complex map of roads and highways. Some of the connections are little more than dirt paths. Others are country roads, and the busiest ones are eight-lane super highways. The skills and behaviors we use most are executed through neural pathways that tend to be highly *myelinated*. Myelin is a substance made of fatty acids and protein that coats our frequently flexed neural pathways and improves the efficiency and speed of electrical impulses moving through them. While we are able to "drive" on the country roads and dirt paths, the commute is slow, and we are more likely to encounter detours. Our brains prefer to stick with tasks and behaviors that can be successfully performed with the least amount of effort.

A Simple Experiment

On a blank sheet of paper, sign your name somewhere in the middle of the page with either a pen or pencil. Pay attention to how easily your hand grabs the writing instrument and executes the task.

After you're done, position your pen a few inches above the original signature, close your eyes and sign your name again. If you're like most people, you will be able to execute the task with the same ease and comfort as you did the first time. The finished product, your signature, probably looks almost identical to your original signature. What's interesting about this experiment is that it shows how efficient our brain can execute a task even when deprived of its most dominant sensory input, vision.

Now, switch your pen or pencil to your non-dominant writing hand, keep your eyes open and sign your name again directly below your original signature. Unless you're ambidextrous, you'll find this task far more difficult to complete even though your eyes are open. More importantly, the task will take longer to execute with poor results when compared to your standard signature. Did you notice the feedback your brain gave you when you forced yourself to execute a task in a manner that you were not efficient? We typically experience a nagging urge to get back to the "right" way of doing things.

As simple as this experiment is, it demonstrates how powerful our current behavior patterns are in influencing how we will respond in the future. It also demonstrates the feedback that our brains generate when we are trying to change behavior. Performing tasks in a new way or training ourselves to respond differently to familiar situations takes more energy, in the form of glucose, for our brains to execute. The reason for this inefficiency is that the brain must create new neural pathways each time it completes a new or infrequently done task.

With our brains having a bias toward sticking with existing neural pathways whenever possible, how do we change behaviors? How do we alter our interaction styles, and the attitudinal orientations that drive our behaviors? The simple answer, while not novel, is to practice. When we practice something, especially when it's driven by motivation to improve, we get better. The trick is to stick with new behaviors long enough that the brain becomes comfortable and proficient with them.

A fascinating topic in the field of brain science is neuroplasticity, the brain's ability to create new physical pathways to support new skills and behaviors. The best news about this topic is that, based on recent research, the human brain remains "plastic" for most people well into their 80s.[12] Contrary to popular belief, old dogs can learn new tricks provided they are interested in learning them!

Another point to keep in mind when trying to develop new behavior patterns is that there will be times when we revert back to our old ways, particularly when under stress. Even when it seems we've turned the corner on past behaviors that got in our way, we sometimes see the remnants of our less flattering patterns emerge. My close friend and colleague Dr. Paul Marciano puts it this way, "Behaviors that change too quickly tend to change back quickly." Even when we occasionally relapse and display behaviors that we know are disrespectful, the best thing to do is quickly apologize if we offended and execute the desired behavior for reinforcement. While some old pathways may never be fully replaced, we can redirect most of the future "traffic" to the desired pathways. Like infrequently traveled dirt roads, when the old neural pathways go unexercised for a long time, they begin to "grow over" and fade away. The brain goes through a process called pruning and gets rid of old pathways that are no longer required.

Respect yourself to better respect others

If we want to bring our best selves into our interactions with others on a consistent basis, then the place to start for most of us is with ourselves. Taking care of ourselves physically, mentally and emotionally makes it more likely that our best selves will be available to others. Even if we are a person who normally treats others with respect, we've all probably had one of those days when our interaction skills were lacking. We cut people off, jump to premature conclusions about their intentions, deliver an uncharacteristically sarcastic comment or roll our eyes in exasperation. Physical energy, stress and how we feel about ourselves all play a significant role in determining our capacity for treating others with respect. Let's take a look at these elements more closely.

Self-Esteem – The Art of Respecting Ourselves

Almost 20 years ago, I remember attending a personal development workshop where the concept of self-esteem was introduced. Even though I'd heard of it before, I had never had the subject thoroughly explained or linked to behavior and performance. The introduction of that subject illuminated for me what I believe to be one of people's greatest blind spots. Healthy self-esteem is not only a reliable predictor of a person's overall mental health and wellness, but also of how they treat others. It is almost impossible to treat other people with respect on a consistent basis unless we respect ourselves first.

Before we define self-esteem, let's make sure we know what it isn't. Over the years, there have been many who have tried to downplay its importance and desirability by linking it to negative attributes such as egotism, arrogance, conceit or a sense of predominance over others. These attitudes, and their related behaviors, are far from those correctly linked to self-esteem, and may actually be indicators of its absence. Because self-esteem is generally thought to have cognitive, affective and behavioral manifestations, let's define it as follows:

Self-esteem is the degree to which individuals feel comfortable with themselves as they are, believe that they have inherent value as individuals, and demonstrate confidence in their ability to successfully achieve their own measure of success.

A person with healthy self-esteem can be characterized as one who has an intrinsic feeling of warm regard for themselves accompanied by a confidence in their ability to successfully navigate their world daily. The adjective *healthy* is intentional in this definition because it suggests a measure of self that is formed not in isolation, but with consideration for others around us. In contrast, there has been research that has linked the condition of *high* self-esteem to attitudes and behaviors such as conceit, bragging, bullying or exploiting others.[13] These are socially undesirable qualities that can damage the productivity of co-workers and the organization overall.

What makes healthy self-esteem so important to our pursuit of respectful treatment of others is that it frees up valuable energy for building mutually healthy relationships. When a person already has a strong emotional core, they expend a relatively small amount of time and effort nurturing their own ego. Because of this, they have more energy available to monitor and support the emotional well-being of those with whom they interact. Even if I value respect for others as a principle, a deficit with my own sense of worth can interfere with my ability to act accordingly.

Healthy self-esteem supports a broad range of attitudes and behaviors that are individually and organizationally beneficial. A few of these include:

- Assuming greater personal accountability for outcomes

- Building and maintaining healthier one-on-one relationships

- Being more receptive to new ideas and other people's approaches

- Demonstrating a greater capacity for empathy

- Comfortably and respectfully interacting with people who have different backgrounds and values

- Respectfully sharing opinions that may run counter to the majority

- Demonstrating socially appropriate levels of assertiveness

- Constructively managing criticism and feedback from others

- Proactively pursuing meaningful goals

- Regularly acknowledging and complimenting the contributions of others

In stark contrast, individuals with unhealthy self-esteem are more prone to perceptions, attitudes and behaviors that hinder their performance and often harm others. They may act in ways that reflect their own low sense of worth in the following ways:

- Accepting poor treatment from others

- Talking disparagingly about themselves or their abilities

- Perpetually waiting for others to tell them what to do

- Demonstrating an excessive need for approval from others

- Greater susceptibility to being talked into decisions or behaviors that would otherwise go against their own values

- Reluctance to share their original ideas or thoughts out of fear of being judged unfavorably by others

- Stated pessimism about their expectations of future success and happiness

Depending on their personality, low self-esteem can also trigger more aggressive behaviors that reflect attempts to make themselves feel superior to others. These often include:

- Propensity to show off or boast about their accomplishments

- Bullying weaker personalities

- Publicly attacking or criticizing others who are viewed as threats

- Gossiping about others in ways that damage their reputation

- Passive aggressive interaction styles

- Unwillingness to be wrong about most topics

- Pattern of hostility toward members of groups that they perceive as different

- Unwillingness to accept feedback on their behaviors from others

A rising tide lifts all boats

Healthy self-esteem at the individual level promotes productive behaviors that can be contagious. Imagine for a moment that your co-workers showed up tomorrow with a slight boost in their level of self-esteem. They feel friendly, engaged and have more confidence in their own knowledge, perceptions and abilities. The effect would be like that of a rising tide in a harbor with many boats. All the boats sit higher, and because of the connectivity that exists between us, something else changes. They aren't just sitting higher in the water; they resonate around each other at a higher, happier and more productive frequency. Given the obvious and observable impact of productivity, how can we get to this place?

Think of healthy self-esteem as a piggy bank that is almost full and the bank's owner as the primary beneficiary. This analogy is appropriate for two reasons. First, the person who owns it is responsible for its balance. Because having healthy self-esteem is a way we think and feel about ourselves, no one else has greater control. Second, other people can influence our esteem balance based on how they engage us. Remember the backpack analogy? If they treat us with respect, they can put a few extra coins into our bank. If they treat us with disrespect, they can take a few out.

Assuming we are the primary guardians of our own esteem, how can we actively work on building and maintaining a healthy balance? The answer lies in a combination of increasing personal awareness, changing some of the stories we tell ourselves and re-evaluating some of the permissions that we give others. In all cases, both the primary power and responsibility for improving the way we feel about ourselves resides with us. Let's take a closer look at some specific techniques we can use in this process.

Eight Steps for Building Respect for Ourselves

1. **Identify the qualities and skills that are most closely linked to your idea of success.**

Current research on self-esteem is conclusive about one point: It is linked to our sense of competence in the areas that are important to us. Specifically, it is linked to our individual perception of success and how well we're performing in its pursuit. For example, if my personal picture of success includes being physically fit, how I feel about myself will be a partial reflection of how I'm doing in this area. Minimally, it will be a reflection of my confidence in whether I believe I can make satisfactory progress in pursuit of my goals.

The most important consideration in this step is to double-check that our definitions of success are our own. We live in a world where people are constantly bombarded with manufactured and polished images of how we should look, dress, socialize, recreate and even make love (cue the erectile dysfunction commercials with waterfalls, coy smiles and bathtubs on the beach at sunset.) If we base our image of success on those offered by pop culture or the media, we risk pinning our emotional well-being to forever changing illusions that are commonly out of our reach. Turn off the noise and tune into yourself. As you look at your current trajectory in life, what is the definition of success that gives you pride and passion in its pursuit?

2. **Identify your current strengths and establish plans for improving your opportunity areas.**

Once you have clarified your personal definition of success, examine where you currently are relative to your desired position.

Figure out what you need to do to make positive adjustments and, as an old friend used to say, "Get after it!" Get off the sofa and get in shape. Spend more quality time with your spouse and/or kids. Change your spending habits and start saving. Grab a laptop and start writing that book. Or, jump on Expedia and look for island resorts that have double-wide bathtubs on a beach. Whatever your goals, there are few things more esteeming than knowing you're making progress towards the goals that match your picture of success.

> *"You have to put in many, many, many tiny efforts that nobody sees or appreciates before you achieve anything worthwhile."*
>
> —Brian Tracy

3. Be on the lookout for new opportunities to grow your talents and experiences.

Growth facilitates vitality and viability. Part of our sense of self-worth comes from the belief and confidence that we have the ability to be successful both today and in the future. Unfortunately, the skills, knowledge and experiences that got us to our current position may not be enough to generate the same results or level of accomplishment tomorrow. We inoculate ourselves against irrelevance by learning anything and everything we can. With a sense of adventure driven by curiosity, make it a point to try one or two new things each month that excite you, and maybe a few that even scare you!

4. Identify and redirect unhealthy competition and comparisons.

If there was one thing I wish my parents had drilled into me more intensely, it would have been to compete not with others, but with myself. Like many, I remember going through grade school and high school trying to keep up with the accomplishments of those around me. Intensified by the competitive nature of an all male high school, I compared myself to others in everything - athletic prowess, academics, social popularity and, of course, dating. While this may have contributed to me becoming fairly proficient at academics and sports, it came at a steep price. My sense of worth was often determined by my view of how well others did. Their accomplishments were sometimes simply more reasons for me to be unhappy with myself.

Foolish as it seems in retrospect, many adults continue to go through life this way. Only the environmental props are different. In the back of their minds, they compare, in relation to their own situation, what they think other people earn and the kind of houses they live in, where they vacation and what cars they drive. They look at what shoes someone wore to the party, who they hang out with and who has the reputation for coming up with the wittiest remarks. They notice who got promoted ahead of them, and whose idea got the most support at the last staff meeting. As personal finance guru Suzy Orman so famously said, "Stop the madness!"

If you look at the unique mix of talent, skills and knowledge each person possesses, no two people are alike. Why, then, would we want to judge ourselves against the accomplishments of others who are fundamentally different from us? Competition drives an invisible wedge between people. It sabotages teamwork and leaves feelings of isolation and alienation. In relation to self-esteem, competition with others hinders control of your own sense of worth. Their failures or shortcomings are your success, and their achievements are your pangs of inadequacy.

It is fine to notice what others accomplish. We are human and that's part of how we determine how we fit in our world. Rather than feeling envy when others are successful, applaud them and, if appropriate, use them as inspiration. Don't forget that their "best" in any particular arena is just that – their best. If you compete with your own best at whatever you do, it is guaranteed that two things will happen. First, you'll fall asleep at night knowing you played the game of life to the best of your abilities that day. Second, tomorrow's best will likely be even better.

5. Forgive yourself for past mistakes and poor decisions.

Having been raised Catholic and then marrying into a Jewish family, there was one constant I have been able to rely upon over the years: guilt. After almost 50 years, I feel certain in saying that, along with its cousin, regret, it is a thoroughly non-productive emotion on which to dwell. While guilt can have a positive impact when it causes us to change or apologize for hurtful behaviors, too many people allow themselves to be held hostage by the mistakes they made weeks, months and even years ago.

From a rational point of view, berating ourselves for past mistakes makes no sense. Whatever we did in the past is in the rearview mirror and can't be undone. Even though it now appears to have been the wrong decision, we believed it was the right thing to do at the time. That's because we complete a level of analysis, quick as it may be, prior to making decisions. Decision-making is a complex process, and sometimes we don't place the correct weight on the right variables. Other times, we don't have all the data available that can lead to better decisions. Finally, sometimes we simply miscalculate the impact of our actions. The point is, we're human, so we need to give ourselves a break on those occasions when we get it wrong.

> *"I am not discouraged, because every wrong attempt discarded is another step forward."*
>
> —Thomas Edison

Being willing and able to forgive yourself for past mistakes accomplishes two important things. First, it frees up amazing amounts of energy that can be spent on current, more productive activities. Second, it breaks the cycle of synaptic reinforcement that reliving past mistakes perpetuates. When we continually replay memories of decisions or behaviors that we now regret, we ironically may be adding more myelin to the neural circuitry that was responsible for the inappropriate actions in the first place. Letting go and moving on is always a more beneficial course of action for all parties involved.

6. Hold yourself completely accountable for your actions, decisions and outcomes.

Is there a legitimate place for short-term guilt and remorse? Yes. As previously mentioned, they are emotional indicators of discomfort that we internally generate when we sense our decisions and behaviors were inappropriate, hurtful or fell short of our own or others' expectations. For guilt to have a positive value, it must lead to some type of behavior change or related correction. If we make a mistake, we need to fix it to the best of our ability. If we complete a project improperly, we go back and do it the way it should have been done. If we damage a relationship, an apology is necessary given in the same venue in which the harm was done. When we consistently improve our personal accountability, it increases our overall sense of effectiveness and competence.

If you are a leader, manager or supervisor, it is critical that you enforce a consistent policy of accountability for everyone who reports to you. If we excuse people who exhibit poor behaviors, disrespectful actions or sub-standard work, it causes multiple damages. Besides what it communicates to others within the organization, failing to hold people accountable may send subtle messages that damage an employee's esteem. It may be interpreted as, "I don't think you can do any better, so I'll accept what is and not expect more." Alternatively, it could signify, "What you were working on isn't that important, so it doesn't matter that you get it right." While ignoring poor behavior or performance may alleviate the potential for short-term conflict, it doesn't promote lasting confidence or competence.

7. Develop a pattern of self talk that validates your worth and abilities.

Each of us has developed a particular way of interpreting and explaining the world around us. This pattern of self-talk is as unique as our fingerprints; we observe and evaluate events, actions and outcomes, and create stories that help us make sense of them. In psychology, the way we stitch these stories together is referred to as our explanatory style. As we observe people behaving in certain ways, and events unfolding in either random or predictable patterns, we evaluate them against three different parameters:

- Was this event or behavior a result of what I did or what one or more others did?

- Is the resulting condition permanent or temporary?

- Do things like this happen all the time, or was this a rare occurrence?

The events, in most cases, are perceived as neutral when viewed by those who were not involved. When they impact us, however, we create a story to evaluate and explain what happened. Are they good or bad? Why did they happen? What are the current and future consequences? This is where our explanatory style comes into play. Consider the following event:

One morning, you arrive at work late due to heavy traffic. You immediately go to the staff meeting that started 10 minutes earlier, quickly apologize for being late and take your seat. Your boss looks directly at you and sarcastically says, "Thanks for gracing us with your presence this morning!" You apologize again and take out your notepad.

How would you "explain" this situation to yourself?

- I'm usually never late, so this is no big deal. He's got a lot on his plate and has a right to be a bit upset, but this will pass. I'll make it up to him somehow later.

- Oh, my God, what have I done? He has it in for me anyway and this is just one more time I've screwed up. I can tell he's really angry and will probably hold this against me during next week's performance review.

- What's the big deal? So I'm 10 minutes late for a meeting. He's been late before and no one yelled at him. What a jerk he is for singling me out like that!

This is the same event with three different interpretations. As it relates to developing and maintaining healthy self-esteem, it's important that our stories neither damage nor free us from blame. Rather, they should cause us to see ourselves as human, prone to occasional short-comings. We should continue to feel worthy, accountable and capable, thus giving us hope for a successful future. More importantly, it is the mindset that allows us to continue to do our best work.

8. Focus on what you can control, not what you can't.

As I've learned the hard way, our short-term destiny is not always in our control. In the early stages of the Great Recession, my business practice faced financial challenges never encountered before. As much as I knew better, it did (albeit temporarily) impact my self-esteem. The clients who raved about my great services still raved. The problem was they weren't calling me to do work. Some clients simply disappeared and weren't quickly being replaced by new prospects. Our 2009 revenue came in at less than half that of the previous year. Even though the rational part of my brain told me that this was an anomaly, the emotional side didn't want to listen. It put up a brave face, but conspiratorially whispered that things might not get better. It invented distorted chains of reasoning that concluded that my dream of a successful business might be over, that I might be a failure. As I'm sure it did for many others, this fear got the best of me for awhile.

Even for someone who knows better, unforeseen and unfamiliar changes in our environments can lead to profoundly unsettling emotional responses. We can't predict what tomorrow will bring, let alone next year. Nor can we reliably predict how we will respond when our environments twist, sometimes cataclysmically, around us. What we can do is make a commitment to do our best in whatever environment we find ourselves. We can also make sure that we build strong friendships with knowledgeable people in advance of us needing their wisdom. As the old adage goes, the best time to replace a roof is always before the storm.

Integrity – The Glue that Holds Respect Together

Whether implied or assumed, there is one "super value" that needs to be embraced for respect to take root within all levels of an organization. That super value is integrity. This element is so essential that without it none of our other actions associated with respect will be viewed as authentic.

To understand the nature of integrity, it is best to first look at it through the lens of things, not people. Think of integrity in terms of design, process and structures. For example, consider a simple steel bolt. By itself, it's both insignificant and harmless. When we use the steel bolt in the construction of a bridge, brake pedal or jet engine, it takes on a whole new level of importance. We assume that it's been, 1) designed and manufactured properly for the application in which it will be used (the right material, hardness and dimensions), 2) will hold together whatever pieces it connects, and 3) will perform reliably under any imaginable condition. We also assume all the pieces around the bolt will do the same. We rely on *every component* used to manufacture an end product to work as expected. When it doesn't, bad things can happen. The failure of one insignificant bolt can weaken an entire structure. If the bolt is in a critical location, it can cause catastrophic failure.

What does it mean when integrity is applied to human systems? First, let's make an important distinction. Integrity is different from morality and ethics. Both these elements involve subjectivity and judgment. Integrity doesn't, at least not in the same way. Moral and ethical conduct implies adherence to a subscribed set of behaviors that have been deemed just and proper for the members of a specific group or community. They can vary from group to group. While mission statements and codes of conduct have an important place in defining cultural norms, what works successfully within one company culture (a law firm, for example), could inhibit optimal performance in another (a hospital system.) In contrast, integrity is more about how consistently the stated moral and ethical expectations are applied within a culture.

> *"The supreme quality for leadership is unquestionable integrity. Without it, no real success is possible, no matter whether it is on a section gang, a football field, in an army, or in an office.*
>
> —Dwight D. Eisenhower

Acting with integrity has several requirements. First, it means that we unconditionally keep or honor our word in all situations. Is there a difference between keeping and honoring? Yes. Sometimes, it becomes impossible to keep a previously made commitment. For example, we promise to attend a meeting on a certain date and time, but can't due to a canceled flight or family emergency. In this case, honoring our word would require that we do the next best thing. This might include arranging a video-conference or immediately rescheduling the meeting regardless of the unexpected costs these actions might involve.

A second requirement for acting with integrity is that we communicate only what we know to be completely true. This does not mean there won't be times when we can't, for legal reasons, share certain elements of what we know. It does mean that we disclose those exceptions when they are present. It also means that we don't allow people to act on assumed information that we know to be false. An example of this would be for a company to continue to promote and sell a product that it knows is unsafe or doesn't perform as advertised.

A third requirement for integrity is that we are clear about our intentions and the reasons behind what we say or do. Related to the previous requirement, this element can be thought of as the "sunshine" clause and involves the transparency of our intentions. If a salesperson recommends a product or service to a client, it should be because it represents the best alternative that he or she can offer to meet the client's needs. If, instead, the recommendation is oriented more toward helping that salesperson win a contest or hit a quota when a better solution is known, then the integrity of the recommendation is in question.

Finally, and perhaps most importantly, integrity requires that we behave in a manner consistent with what we believe to be "right." This includes meeting stakeholder's expectations. If I am a financial advisor, this means I act in the best interests of my investor clients. If I am a doctor, I make recommendations and suggestions that I believe to be in my patients' best interest. Doing what we believe to be right, even when others around us don't, is one of the most courageous gestures we can make in the name of integrity.

Arguably, the right thing in any specific situation can be subject to different interpretations based on the competing standards and expectations of various groups of stakeholders. For example, most fast-food restaurants market and sell products they know are inherently unhealthy due to saturated fats, highly processed carbohydrates and caloric density. One could argue that, from the perspective of consumers, it is wrong to sell any products that are scientifically or medically proven to be harmful. On the other hand, anyone who owns stock in these companies rightfully expects that their leaders are doing everything in their collective power to grow revenue and profits. If there is a grey area in determining what is right and what isn't, this is the place. If we are committed to integrity, we are required to make the decisions that impact the majority of our stakeholders favorably. Otherwise, we need to be clear in our communications if we pursue the best outcomes for one particular group over another.

Why is integrity such a significant component of respectful work cultures? At the personal level, the perception of integrity in our actions reinforces the belief in others that they are valued and important. It supports the notion that their ability to work in a predictable environment that takes their well-being into consideration is the primary value guiding our conduct around them. The direct result of this perception is trust, and some level of trust must exist through our interactions with others if we are to reach the state of respect.

The higher our position within the organization, the more impactful this trust dividend becomes. That's because it sets the tone for our superiors and subordinates. Culture trickles down in an organization, and leadership behaviors set the tone for everyone else. As powerful as personal integrity is for enabling individual engagement, systemic integrity can become a strategic asset. It helps lead to a platform of trust and predictability that encourages an entire organization to engage.

PART

III

"*The best thing to give to your enemy is forgiveness; to an opponent, tolerance; to a friend, your heart; to your child, a good example; to a father, deference; to your mother, conduct that will make her proud of you; to yourself, respect; to all men, charity.*"

~ Benjamin Franklin

The Path Forward

A Blueprint for Respectful Organizations

Over the past decade, I have worked with dozens of organizations to help them map out the strategy, resource requirements and tools for building and sustaining respectful workplaces. Some were large, Fortune 50, others were small, most were for-profit and some were not. The one thing almost all the organizations recognized early was that focusing on respect wasn't a time constrained initiative. It was a long-range, cultural aspiration to be pursued and protected with the same consistency and energy as any other strategic asset. One client explained it best the following way:

> "Our organization has four core values. Each is important, but we tend to focus on one or two more consistently than the others. For example, if you were to ask any of our employees or our customers if we are a *safe* company, we consistently see that over 99% of those asked the question responded with a yes. Safety has been ingrained as a part of our culture for over 100 years. But if you were to ask them if we are a respectful company, the response would be a bit lower. It wouldn't be low, maybe 80% yes, but it wouldn't be as high as safety.

Does this mean we have a problem with respect in our organization? Not at all. It simply means that we have not focused on respect nearly as much as we have safety. You can think of it as a four-legged stool where one or two of the legs are significantly longer than the others. It doesn't make for a very stable platform. Because of the business benefits that we know exist from its pursuit, our long-term goal is for our employees and customers to think of us as a respectful place to work (and vendor with whom to work) just as much as they do a safe place to work."

In order to create a more respectful workplace, there are three distinct gates that must be passed through to make it happen. They are the same three gates that are required for the success of any cultural initiative.

Gate One: Mapping

I once heard my college professor observe, "If you don't know where you're going, any road will take you there." To become a more respectful workplace, it is crucial that you determine your starting point. The only way to gauge the current perceptions of your employees is to ask them. The traditional method for doing this is through surveys. Surveys don't need to be long to be effective. They do need to ask the right questions. It is important that the responses be evaluated in a way that highlights the current perceptions and also explains them. For example, a typical survey question on this topic might read as follows: *"My manager or supervisor treats all of his or her subordinates equally."* While the responses to this question can be illuminating, it might not provide enough information to be acted upon.

The best survey providers perform regression analysis on the responses. This simply means that they try to establish relationships between the response patterns. For example, the responses to the above question might correlate positively to the answers for this question: *"My manager takes the time to get to know me as an individual."* This would suggest that how a supervisor treats subordinates is influenced by perceptions of how much time he or she spends getting to know each employee. This may give the impression of getting lost in the details, but this level of analysis is crucial because it helps determine future intervention strategies designed to help raise scores.

Another tool to help understand current perceptions is 360° feedback surveys for senior leaders, managers and supervisors. It is worth repeating that they are unparalleled in their ability to generate accurate, actionable feedback for individuals responsible for leading others. To effectively try to lead a group or organization without knowing how you are perceived is analogous to driving a race car at night while wearing sunglasses. You better have good insurance!

Gate Two: The Invitation

Following the collection of metrics, senior leadership is responsible for crafting and delivering the vision. To do this, they need to invite their employees to become co-creators of a more respectful workplace. The key elements of this invitation need to answer the following questions for employees:

- What are we doing?

- Why are we doing it (how will this make us better)?

- When is this going to happen?

- What resources will be allocated for this effort?

- Who will be involved?

- How will this affect me?

- What will be expected from me?

To avoid getting lost in the technical elements of communication strategy, it's important that senior leadership, preferably the CEO, share his or her vision regarding the importance of a respectful workplace. This includes why it is vital to the long-term success of the organization. Senior leadership should lay out the plan for how the vision will be achieved, including the different mile markers along the journey. The message needs to be delivered with humility. If the effort is perceived as just another "program of the month," the journey may take longer or not be fruitful. The effort put into this phase can serve as a commitment checkpoint. If every member of the senior leadership team can't be counted on to participate, walk the talk and be open to feedback, this may serve as an indication that the organization isn't ready to embrace an initiative of this nature.

Gate Three: Cultivation

Assuming there are no casualties up to this point, the real work begins. In order for rich, pervasive and enduring respect to take root, the field must be cultivated and the seeds planted. Cultivation takes place on different levels, and eventually needs to touch everyone in the organization. The logical starting place is leadership and management. Based on feedback from whatever survey tools were deployed, leaders and key managers need to create action plans to address the identified gaps. The tools used in these plans may include focus groups, communication campaigns and use of outside consultants. This also includes training for leaders, managers and individual contributors.

Cultivation requires a proven methodology, attention to detail, patience, vigilance for obstacles and a feedback loop to chart progress. The tools used are typically deployed repeatedly, including surveys to check the pulse of the organization, focus groups to understand the nuance of survey results, and training to educate and reinforce the focus.

"It takes less time to do the right thing than to explain why you did it wrong."

—Henry Wadsworth Longfellow

Training is used as a vehicle for instruction and for building collaboration. One example is the creation of a Code of Cooperation. This exercise is designed to give employees who work together a greater voice in determining the behavioral norms that define their interpretation of what a respectful workplace should look like. While there may be general guidelines that everyone must follow, like the organization's existing code of conduct or ethics policies, each group's Code of Cooperation document reflects the personality of its creators. The trade-off with this method of formalizing behavioral norms is between consistency and adherence. While it's assumed there may be variations between Codes of Cooperation created by different groups within an organization, the likelihood that these documents will be supported goes up exponentially because of their unique content. People support what they help create. Giving a group the ability to have a voice in defining what respect should look like increases their accountability over time.

Cultivating Respect as a Global Asset

Corporate giant E. I. DuPont De Nemours and Company (DuPont), the Delaware based diversified manufacturer, has four core values. The first three are safety, exhibiting the highest ethical standards and protecting the environment. When they included respect for people as the fourth, they were on to something. DuPont realized a long time ago that if you respect your people they will respect each other, produce at a higher level and improve in the other three core values. For those reasons, respect has been a company core value for years. While there may be a peripheral impact on profits and litigation avoidance, these are coincidental. DuPont leadership believes it's the right way to run a successful company.

According to Greg Martz, Director of Respect for People Central, "Though we had a diverse, inclusive work environment, our other core values had more structure, systemized improvement programs, and dedicated resources. Respect for People was trailing in its formal approach." In 2009 DuPont's senior leadership decided to do something about it.

The effort started by surveying over 13,000 of DuPont's 58,000 employees in 69 discovery locations. The results of this enormous undertaking showed that close to 90 percent of those surveyed believed that DuPont was a respectful place to work. That would be a satisfactory mark for many organizations but in terms of a core value within DuPont, 90 percent left room for improvement. They knew they needed training, audit capabilities, metrics and communications processes.

With the aid of Legacy Business Cultures, who helped with the creation of a customized training curriculum,

DuPont trained over 200 facilitators worldwide by the summer of 2011. DuPont is committed to delivering respect training in 25 languages to more than 40,000 employees by 2014. Senior leadership at DuPont fully supports the effort and is providing the resources, funding and promotion a major corporate roll out needs to be successful.

Along with the training, DuPont is also creating internal communications programs that help generate more knowledge about respect. DuPont is convinced the effort they are championing will make it a better place to work and provide a positive bottom line return. That's good news for both employees and the company's shareholders.[14]

Don't Expect Perfection

Just like the proverbial road to hell is paved with good intentions, the road to respect occasionally finds itself in need of repair. Potholes, obstacles and detours can be expected. Competitive threats, financial obstacles, technology shifts and the occasional leaders who don't grasp the "people thing" will sometimes put culture in the backseat.

The good news is that the cultural norms that resonate best for most people tend to be enduring. Whether they are respect, integrity, safety or customer focus, some values and their associated behaviors simply lead to stronger, smarter and more adaptable businesses.

When it Doesn't Work, Throw it Out

Dealing with deeply-entrenched cultural challenges often requires more than a good strategy and the right tools. Sometimes, you need a broom first. Such was the case with an international electronics manufacturer. When the new Manager of Sales Training was hired, he was consoled by some of his peers. It seems his group had a reputation for being hard to work with. Associates wished him luck, and he soon found out he was going to need it.

The first few months on the job were rough. Staff meetings were dysfunctional, people routinely showed up late and hostility between key members of the team was normal. Efforts to exert some sort of control and positive influence over the group were only marginally successful and the group's overall productivity was poor. At one point, the manager found himself being pulled into the drama he inherited and "lost it" during a meeting. Something had to change.

That watershed moment proved to be the catalyst for change that was needed to propel the manager onto a different path. It became clear that some of the relationships between his key reports were too badly damaged to be repaired. The disrespect demonstrated between them wasn't just "surface rust." The years of neglect and the corrosive attitudes and behaviors had resulted in structural damage that the key players themselves weren't even interested in fixing. The resulting toxicity rubbed off on everyone with the by-products of low group morale, projects that took far too long to complete and mediocre quality of programming.

The key players knew there was a problem, but they were too stuck to move on their own. The manager met with each one individually to see where their hearts were. During these non-threatening and reflective meetings, they concluded that they weren't where they needed to be for either their personal or the team's success. Each employee independently decided it was time for a change. No tearful terminations, no expensive severance packages and more importantly, no animosity.

The message to the remaining team members was clear. The old behavioral norms weren't acceptable. The group's work on behalf of the company was too important to be compromised by people who either couldn't or wouldn't work well together. Mutual respect, a positive attitude and accountability became the new cultural norms and performance flourished within months.

Respect Outside of Work

As important as the pursuit of respect is in the global workplace, it is no less important in our homes and communities. The two really can't be separated if there is to be any sustainable change in the former. I am sure I'm not the first to notice that respect and civility seem to be taking a back seat to expediency in our high-tech, high-volume society. You can sense it in our interaction styles, the "in your face" behaviors glamorized on our television shows and, regrettably, in the increasingly negative tone of our political discourse. The same "neural mathematics" that determines workplace productivity also dictates the output and accomplishments of societies and nations. Energy that is spent criticizing, demeaning and otherwise tearing down our fellow citizens is energy that can't be spent to build.

Family and friends

Any book focusing on the use of respect to leverage culture, emotions and neuroscience to build a better business wouldn't be complete without addressing what happens when employees leave the office. Long work days, busy extra-curricular schedules, dual career paths and "smart" devices in people's pockets can hinder engaged, respectful home environments. Nostalgia aside, something seems to have been lost from the family experience over the past few decades. On the decrease is the undivided, one-on-one attention that we used to give each other. Some will say that this is an over-broad generalization; that attention gaps of various names have existed in every modern society. To this observer, it appears we are hell-bent on multi-tasking ourselves right out of the respect, curiosity and thoughtfulness that have been the hallmarks of civilized society for thousands of years.

I remember as a child on the late 60s how frustrated my mother would get with my father. No matter how much she pleaded, she found it almost impossible to convince him to participate in a family dinner without the evening news playing on his 12-inch, Sylvania black and white television set. Even then, the hypnotic pull of television competed for the attention of those sitting just a few feet away from us and frequently won. Today, that competition is all but over. No matter what the venue, the familiar glow of televisions and smart phones can be seen intruding upon and interrupting almost every venue for social interaction. Restaurants, theaters, kitchen tables, living rooms, elevators, passenger seats and night stands are all fair game. It has been with some amusement that I've seen people sneaking a peak at their mobile devices in houses of worship and restrooms. I suspect that it's only a matter of time before our most private encounters are routinely interrupted by our favorite songs and ringtones and we won't think twice about whether or not it's okay to respond.

Far from shunning technology, I say let's embrace it with boundaries. When we talk with our spouses, partners, kids or friends, let's do it face-to-face whenever possible, without our trigger fingers waiting for the first hint of vibration from our pocket. Let's make time to connect with those closest to us. Whether over dinner, family outings or simple walks around the block, let's commit to validating each other by sharing the two commodities for which there are no surrogates - time and attention. With two pre-teen children, I'll be the first to admit that I still need some practice when it comes to being fully present in my family interactions. I'm hoping that intention will at least nudge me in the right direction.

There are several reasons why it is important that we display respect and civility with our family and friends. First, those closest to us deserve our absolute best. Second, remember the paths our brains form from repeated behaviors? Being consistently respectful both at work and home reinforces the positive behaviors we strive to make permanent. The more we practice civility the greater the chance it becomes second nature in every aspect of our lives. Finally, because of our close relationships, our family and friends are probably more forgiving than our employers and co-workers. That doesn't mean that my wife (or my children) should expect less attention and respect from me than I give my employees.

Our political dialogue

Nowhere is the insidious creep of incivility and disrespect more apparent than in our political processes. And nowhere besides the workplace is the need for respect greater. What used to be subtle, ideological and/or philosophical differences have been replaced with stark, inflexible labels. What used to be known as political discourse and debate have been replaced with villainization, smear tactics and outright lying. While the short-term victims of the tactics of negativity are the decent candidates and ideas that fall victim to it, the long-term victims are "we the people."

Research shows that negative political ads work amazingly well. They are effective because of how our brains process information.[15] Negative messages are designed to evoke the powerful emotions of fear, anger and disdain, and attach them to a potential candidate or issue. A barrage of negative messages from multiple angles and toward numerous targets is emotionally draining and may cause people to disconnect from the political process. Rather than increasing participation in democracy, negativity and incivility actually threaten democracy and send it in a downward spiral.

Is there a place for critique and the healthy competition of ideas and ideologies that will determine the future of our countries? Of course there is. In fact, the bedrock of our democratic principles is our ability to present differing visions and priorities for our future. In the increasingly Darwinian environment of super PACs, almost limitless campaign contributions and 24/7 news coverage, the goal is for a candidate or position to win. As the political arena becomes progressively more uncivil, hopefully people will notice, grow tired of these tactics and simply tune out the messages of fear and anger.

Respect is about me

All paths we take toward others eventually circle back to ourselves. Even if you personally make the commitment to practice respect, not everyone you meet will do the same. Some won't take the time and energy necessary to engage you or find common ground on issues. Others may not demonstrate that they value you as a person. They'll show up late for important meetings, interrupt you while you speak and harshly criticize your ideas without being brave enough to offer their own. There will be those who occasionally yell and use vulgar language, attack you personally and lie. There are also individuals who will say or do things we interpret as disrespectful not out of malice or spite, but simply out of ignorance. When we commit to a path of respect, we do so in spite of these eventualities because it reflects who we are at our core.

> *"Thousands of candles can be lighted from a single candle, and the life of the candle will not be shortened. Happiness never decreases by being shared."*
>
> —Hermann Hesse, Siddhartha

Respect is about you and me, not "them," and our commitment to it influences everyone around us. Once we understand the value proposition respect offers, that insight can provide us with patience, courage and creativity. Patience permits us to maintain our composure and respectful demeanor when others are not acting at their best. Courage enables us to candidly challenge disrespectful behaviors and actions directed toward others. Creativity allows us to see points of connection, even in the midst of conflict. When we bring these qualities on-line and into our work interactions, everyone benefits, including our peers, customers, vendors and ultimately, our shareholders.

Once again, I think back to my college friend Dale and am thankful that he showed me respect even when I didn't necessarily deserve it. In retrospect, he likely did so as much for himself as he did for me; it was simply an active demonstration to himself of the person he chose to be. I just happened to be a lucky recipient. I'd also like to think that his commitment to himself paid future dividends through me to my current colleagues and others that he'll never meet.

Final Thoughts

Emotions are triggered in the blink of an eye and by the subtlest of cues. Their impact on our performance is profound and sometimes lasting. I've been the receiver of respect many times over and benefited from its afterglow. I've also tasted my share of disrespect and been sent into a downward spiral of anger, frustration, fear or apathy. Simply paying attention to how other's behaviors impact us can help to keep our awareness of our own behaviors in clearer focus. It also reminds us how inextricably linked to each other we will always be.

Just as there are many reasons compelling us to elevate respect to a higher level of social and professional importance, there are many obstacles that get in our way. Time pressures, competing agendas, lack of awareness, our sometimes low sense of self-worth or physical exhaustion can all cloud our ability to treat each other with the respect and dignity we deserve. Unfortunately, the costs of these short-comings to business are great. Lawsuits, low productivity, high turnover, poor customer satisfaction and diminished resilience are just the tip of the iceberg. The bottom-line impact of diminished physical health, compromised trust and stifled creativity may never be fully appreciated.

With so much at stake, why would any business or society not strive to get better? The simple reason is inertia. Change is difficult, self-interest more convenient and the status quo far easier to maintain. This in no way means that change is impossible. If it were not, humans would never have made it as far as they have. Nor does it mean that we can let ourselves off the hook from trying. To the contrary, the battle for respect is very winnable and more than pays for itself in increased shareholder value. For many organizations, it already has. There are numerous examples of companies who have made great progress in their pursuit of respect with healthier bottom lines to show for it. What's holding you back from joining them?

"Never doubt that a small group of thoughtful, committed people can change the world. Indeed, it is the only thing that ever has."

—Margaret Mead

References

Abrashoff, Michael. *It's Your Ship*. New York: Warner Books, 2002.

Babauta, Leo. *The Power of Less*. New York: Hyperion, 2009.

Bloom, Paul. *How Pleasure Works*. New York: W.W. Norton & Company, Inc., 2010.

Branden, Nathaniel. *How to Raise Your Self-Esteem*. New York: Bantam Books, 1988.

Cozolino, Louis J. *The Neuroscience of Human Relationships, Attachment And The Developing Social*

Brain. W. W. Norton & Company, Inc., 2007.

Davidson, Martin. *The End Of Diversity As We Know It*. San Francisco: Berrett-Koehler Publishers, Inc., 2011.

Doidge, Norman. *The Brain That Changes Itself*. Penguin Group USA, 2008.

Dourado, Phil. *The 60 Second Leader*. New York: MJF Books, 2007.

Ferrazzi, Keith. *Never Eat Alone*. New York: Currency Doubleday, 2005.

Ferrazzi, Keith. *Who's Got Your Back*. New York: Broadway Books, 2009.

Finkelstein, Sydney. *Why Smart Executives Fail*. New York: Portfolio, 2004.

Gladwell, Malcolm. *Blink: The Power of Thinking Without Thinking*. Little, Brownard Company, 2005.

Goldsmith, Marshall. *What Got You Here Won't Get You There*. New York, NY: Hyperion, 2007.

Goleman, Daniel. *Working with Emotional Intelligence*. Bantam, 1998.

Goleman, Daniel. *Emotional Intelligence: Why It Can Matter More Than IQ*. Bantham, 2006.

Gonthier, Giovenella & Morrissey, Kevin. *Rude Awakenings: Overcoming the Civility Crisis in the*

Workplace. Kaplan Business, 2002.

Gostick, Adrian & Chester, Elton. *The Carrot Principle*. New York, NY: Free Press, 2007.

Hallowell, MD, Edward. *Shine*. Boston, MA: Harvard Business Review Press, 2011.

Heath, Chip & Dan. *Made to Stick*. New York: Random House, 2007.

Hsieh, Tony. *Delivering Happiness*. New York: Grand Central Pub, 2010.

Johnson, Thomas. *Relevance Regained*. New York Toronto New York: Free Press Maxwell Macmillan

Canada Maxwell Macmillan International, 1992.

Kabachnick, Terri. *I Quit But Forgot to Tell You.* Cornerstone Leadership Institute, 2006.

Kotter, John & Heskett, James. *Corporate Culture and Performance.* New York, NY: The Free Press, 1992.

Lancaster, Lynne. *When Generations Collide.* Harper Collins, 2002.

Marciano, Paul. *Carrots and Sticks Don't Work.* McGraw-Hill Professional, 2011.

Marsh, Jason; Rodolfo Mendoza-Denton & Smith, Jeremy. *Are We Born Racist?* Boston, MA: Beacon Press, 2010.

Medina, John. *Brain Rules.* Seattle, WA: Peer Press, 2008.

Miller, Marc. *A Seat at the Table.* Austin, Tex: Greenleaf Book Group Press, 2009.

Moawad, Bob & Hoisington,TJ. *The Secret of the Slight Edge.* New York: Aviva Publishing, 2007.

Olver, Kim & Baugh, Sylvester. *Leveraging Diversity at Work.* Country Club Hills: Inside Out Press, 2006.

Patterson, Kerry; Grenny, Joseph; McMillan, Ron & Switzler, Al. *Crucial Conversations.* Teach Yourself, 2003.

Pink, Daniel. *Drive, The Surprising Truth About What Motivates Us.* New York: Riverhead Books, 2009.

Ramsey, Dave. *Entreleadership.* New York: Howard Books, 2011.

Rath, Tom & Clifton, Donald. *How Full is Your Bucket?* New York: Gallup Pr, 2004.

Restak, M.D., Richard. *The Naked Brain*. New York: Three Rivers Press, 2006.

Roizen, Michael & Oz, Mehmet. *You Being Beautiful: The Owner's Manual to Inner and Outer Beauty*.

New York: Free Press, 2008.

Sanders, Tim. *The Likeability Factor*. New York: Three Rivers Press, 2006.

Seligman, Martin. *What You Can Change and What You Can't*. Knopf, 1993.

Senge, Peter. *The Fifth Discipline*. Currency Doubleday, 1990.

Szollose, Brad. *Liquid Leadership*. Austin, Tex: Greenleaf Book Group, 2011.

Taylor, Lynn. *Tame Your Terrible Office Tyrant (TOT)!* Hoboken, N.J: Wiley, 2009.

Thompson, Henry. *The Stress Effect*. San Francisco : Jossey-Bass, 2010.

Walters, Ronald. *Freedom Is Not Enough*. Rowman & Littlefield Publishers, 2007.

Washington, Denzel. *A Hand to Guide Me*. Des Moines, Iowa: Meredith Books, 2006.

Weiss, Joseph. *Organizational Behavior and Change*. Minneapolis/St. Paul: West Pub. Co., 1996.

West, Cornel. *Race Matters.* Beacon Press, 1993.

Whitney, John. *The Trust Factor.* McGraw Hill, 1994.

Zukav, Gary & Francis, Linda. *The Heart of the Soul – Emotional Awareness.* Simon & Schuster Source, 2001.

ENDNOTES

1. Daniel Goleman, *Primal Leadership*. (Harvard Business Review Press; 1 edition March 15, 2002)

2. Jason Marsh, Rodolfo Mendoza-Denton & Jeremy Adam Smith. *Are We Born Racist? New Insights from Neuroscience and Positive Psychology*. (Copyright 2010 by Beacon Press)

3. Adrienne Fox (quote by Ellen Weber), HR Magazine: *The Brain at Work* http://www.shrm.org/Publications/hrmagazine/EditorialContent/Pages/3Fox-Your%20Brain%20on%20the%20Job.aspx (March 1, 2008)

4. Gallup, *Employee Engagement: A Leading Indicator of Financial Performance*. http://www.gallup.com/consulting/52/employee-engagement.aspx

5. Dr. Paul Marciano, *Carrots & Sticks Don't Work*. (McGraw-Hill; 1 edition, June 14, 2010)

6. Roizen, Michael & Oz, Mehmet. *You Being Beautiful: The Owner's Manual to Inner and Outer Beauty*. (Copyright 2008 by Free Press)

7. *Sucking Up to the Boss May Move You Up and Keep You Healthy.* Science Daily http://www.sciencedaily.com/releases/2011/06/110609112426.htm (June 9, 2011)

8. Robert A. Burton, *On Being Certain-Believing You Are Right Even When You're Not.* (Copyright 2008 by St. Martin's Press)

9. *What is Servant Leadership?* http://www.greenleaf.org/whatissl/

10. *Forty-seven percent of Americans think gay is a life choice,* http://open.salon.com/blog/gaypersonsofcolor/2009/12/18/forty-seven_percent_of_americans_think_gay_is_a_life_choice (Dec. 18, 2009)

11. Jason Marsh, Rodolfo Mendoza-Denton & Jeremy Adam Smith. *Are We Born Racist? New Insights from Neuroscience and Positive Psychology.* (Copyright 2010 by Beacon Press.)

12. Paris Achen. *Aging Brains Can Still be Growing Brains. Live Well.* The Columbian. http://www.columbian.com/news/2012/jan/22/aging-brains-can-still-be-growing-brains/ (January 22, 2012)

13. *No Difference in Women's and Men's Self-Esteem in Youth and Early Adulthood, Study Finds.* Science Daily http://www.sciencedaily.com/releases/2011/07/110714120714.htm (July 15, 2011)

14. Courtesy Legacy Business Cultures. (Copyright 2011)

15. Ruthann Lariscy, *Why Negative Political Ads Work.* http://www.cnn.com/2012/01/02/opinion/lariscy-negative-ads/index.html (Jan. 2, 2012)